# TOP 50

## movie & tv classics

### Arranged by Dan Coates

**Alfred**

Produced by
Alfred Music
P.O. Box 10003
Van Nuys, CA 91410-0003
**alfred.com**

Produced in USA.

ISBN-10: 0-7390-7786-4
ISBN-13: 978-0-7390-7786-3

Cover image: CINEMA painted on a brick wall © iStockphoto.com / mayracjp

# TABLE OF CONTENTS

# AS TIME GOES BY

(from *Casablanca*)

Words and Music by Herman Hupfeld
Arranged by Dan Coates

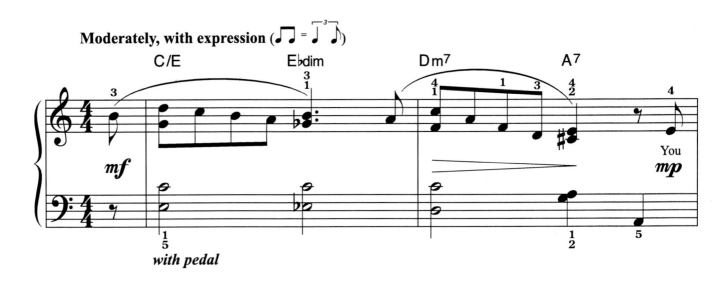

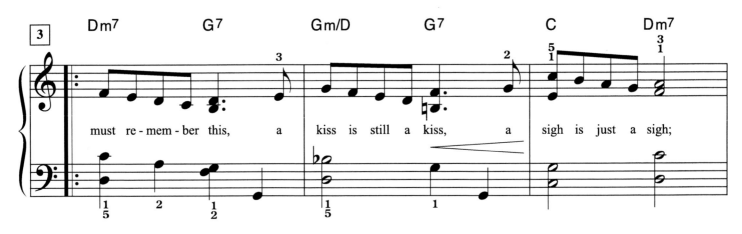

must re-mem-ber this, a kiss is still a kiss, a sigh is just a sigh;

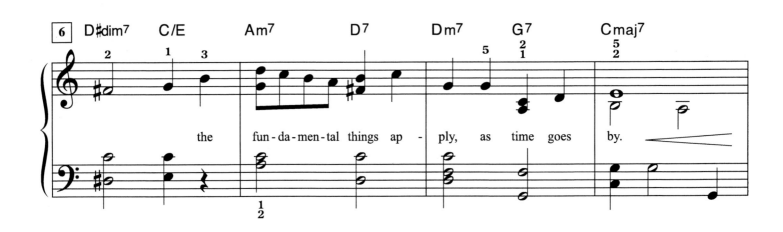

the fun-da-men-tal things ap-ply, as time goes by.

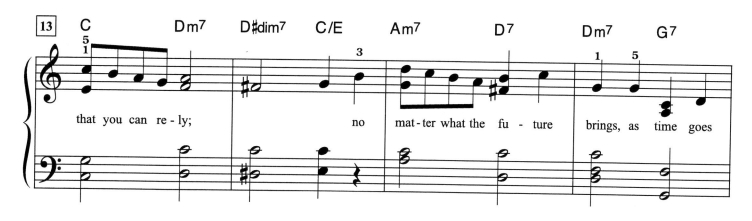

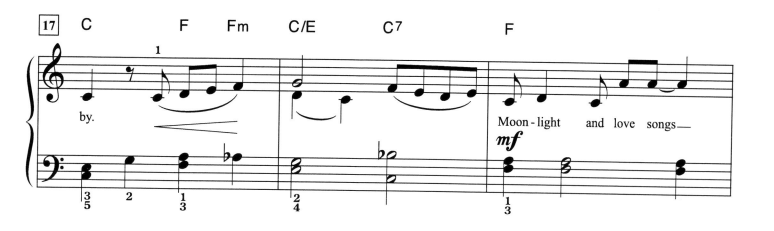

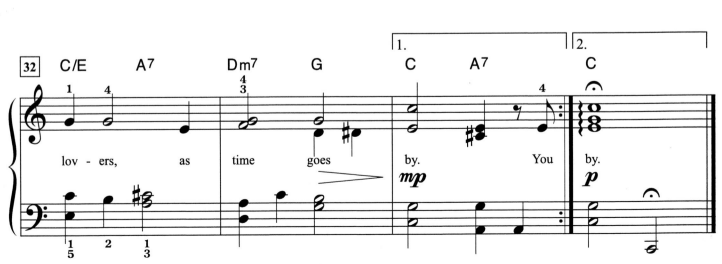

# THE BALLAD OF GILLIGAN'S ISLAND

(from *Gilligan's Island*)

Words and Music by
Sherwood Schwartz and George Wyle
Arranged by Dan Coates

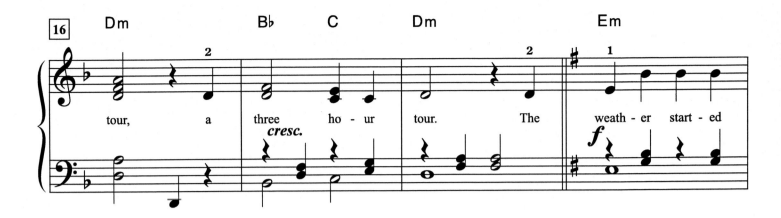

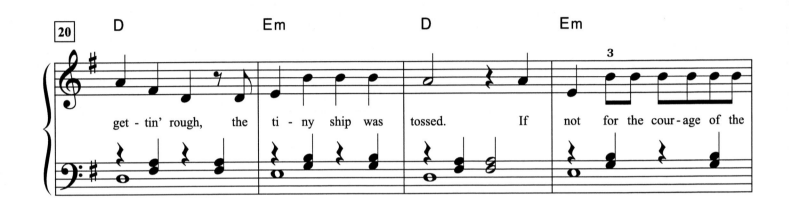

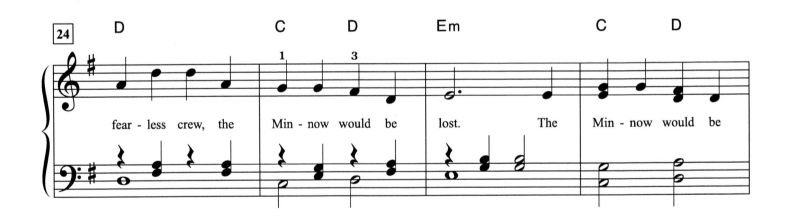

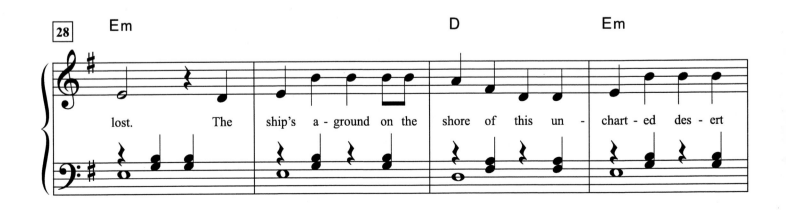

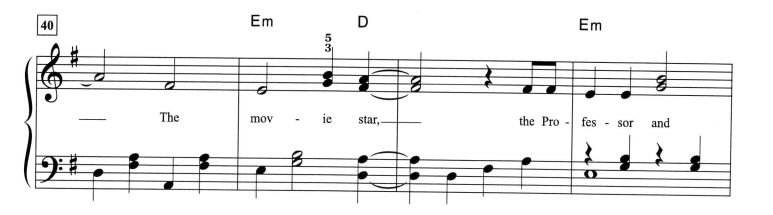

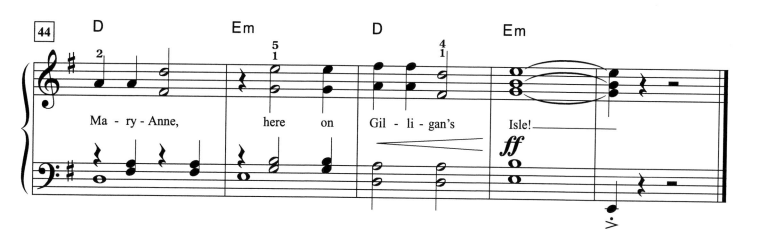

# BATMAN THEME

Words and Music by Neal Hefti
Arranged by Dan Coates

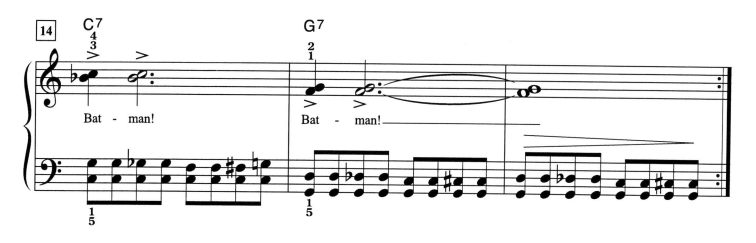

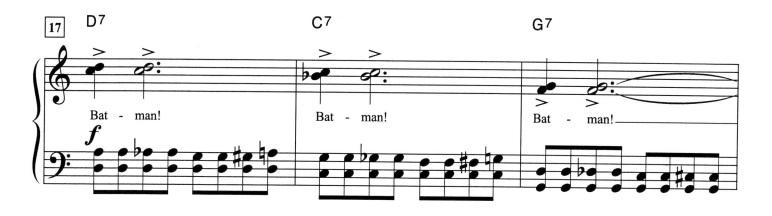

# THE BIG BANG THEORY

## (Main Title Theme)

Words and Music by Ed Robertson
Arranged by Dan Coates

# CAN YOU FEEL THE LOVE TONIGHT

### (from Walt Disney's *The Lion King*)

Music by Elton John
Words by Tim Rice
Arranged by Dan Coates

14

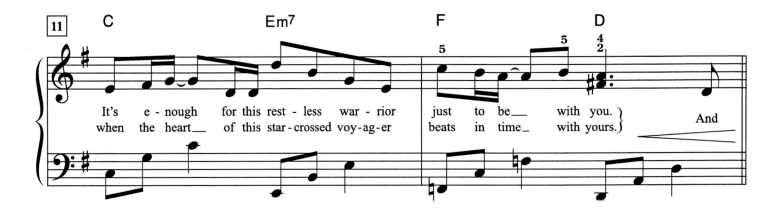

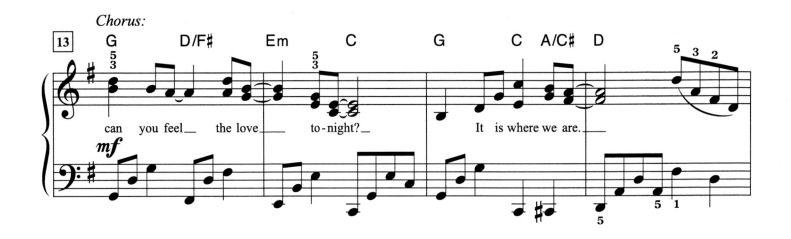

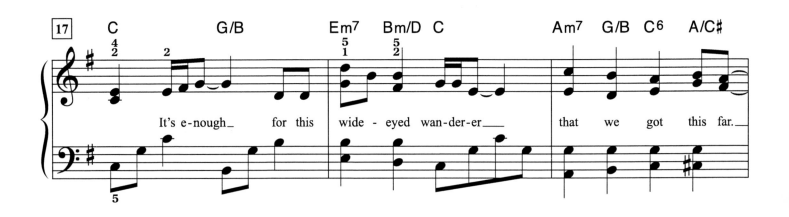

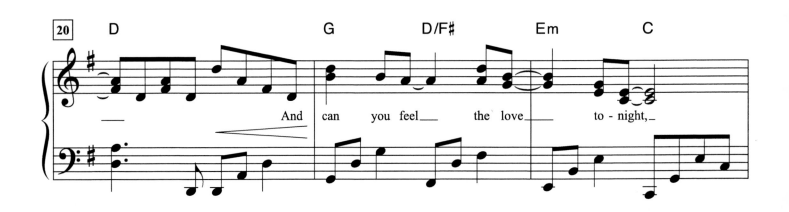

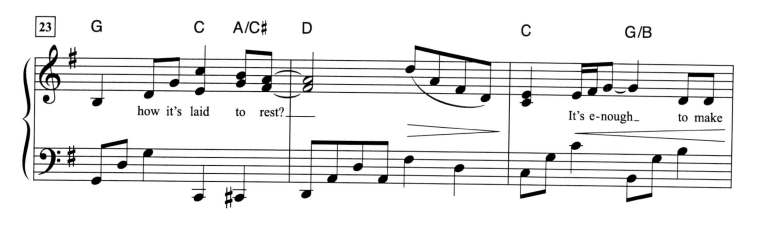

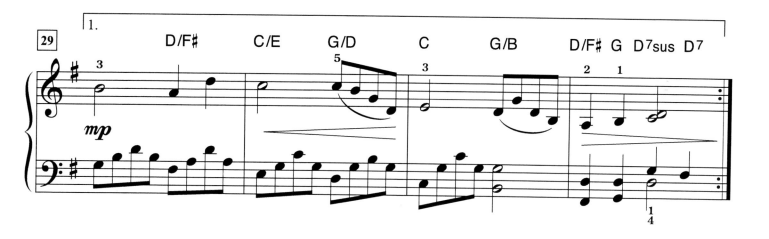

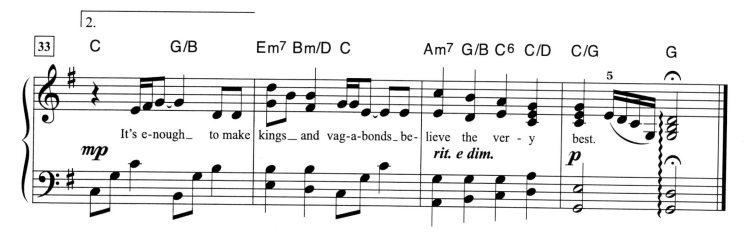

# CANTINA BAND

## (from *Star Wars Episode IV: A New Hope*)

Music by John Williams
Arranged by Dan Coates

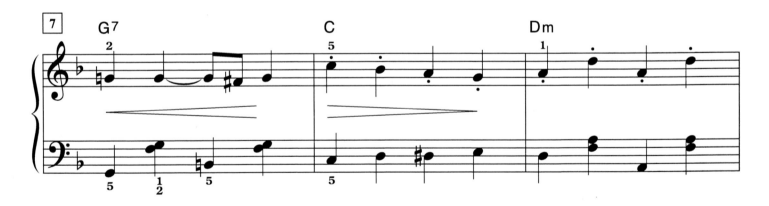

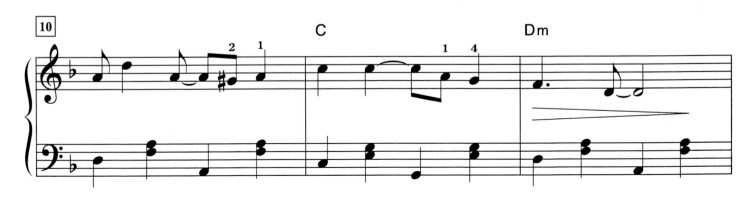

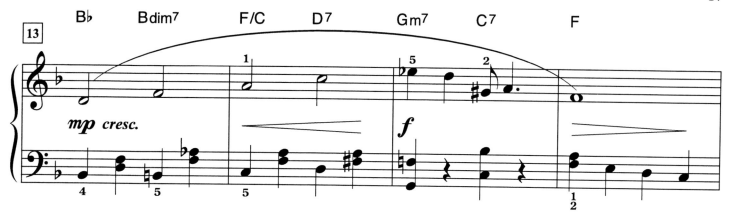

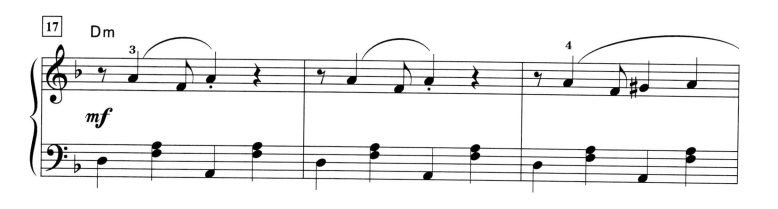

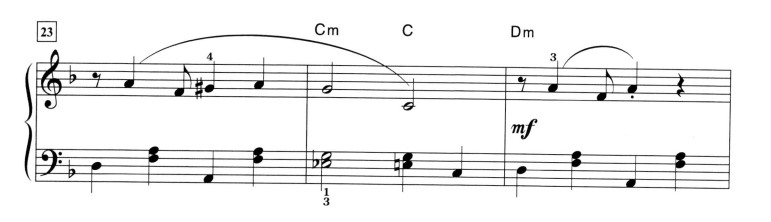

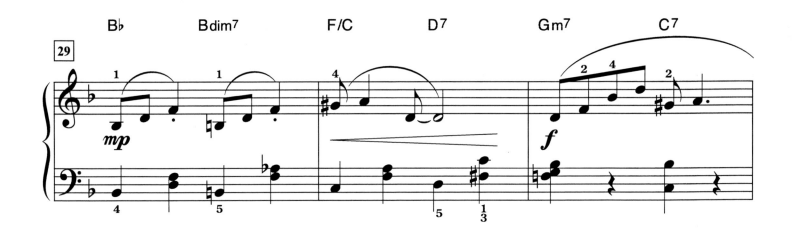

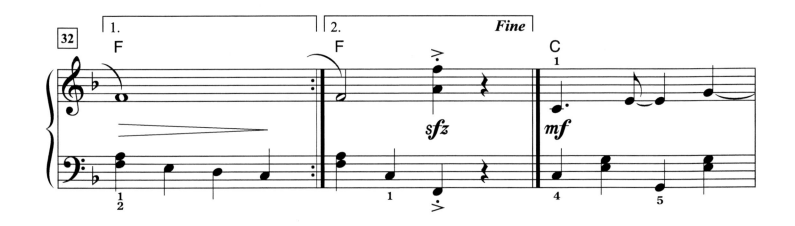

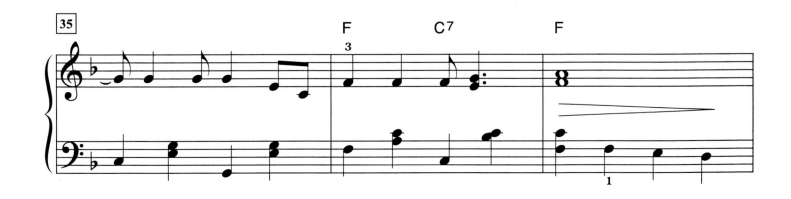

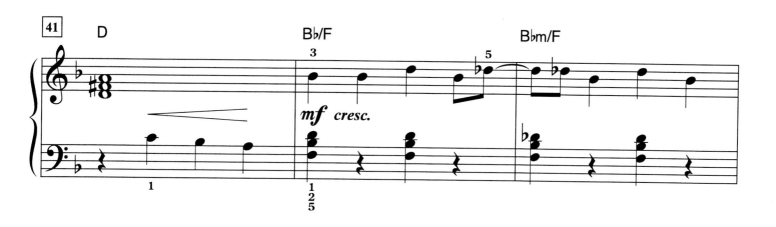

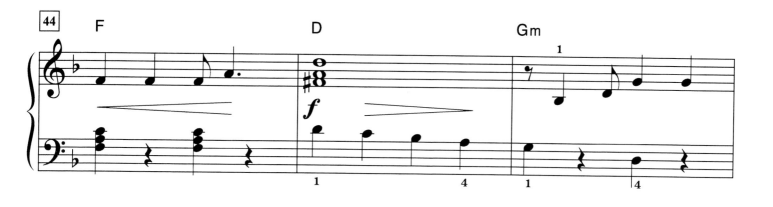

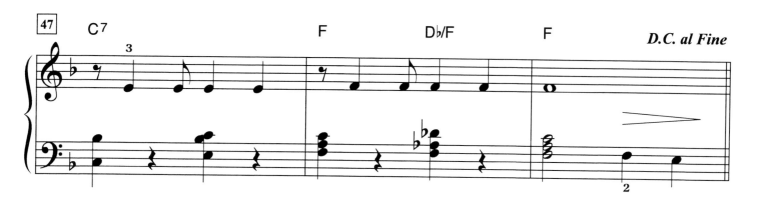

# COLORS OF THE WIND

(from Walt Disney's *Pocahontas*)

Lyrics by Stephen Schwartz
Music by Alan Menken
Arranged by Dan Coates

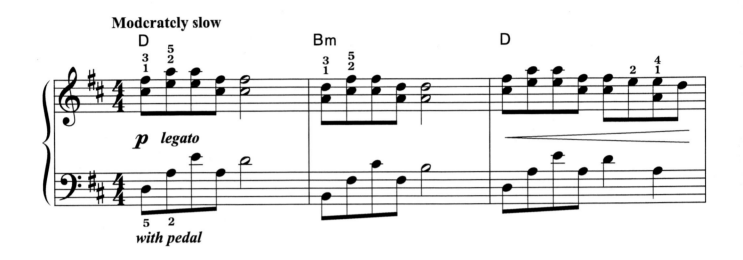

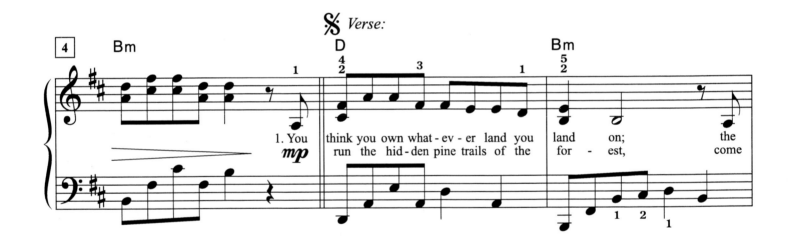

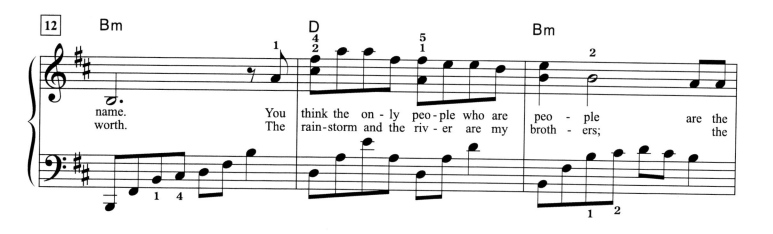

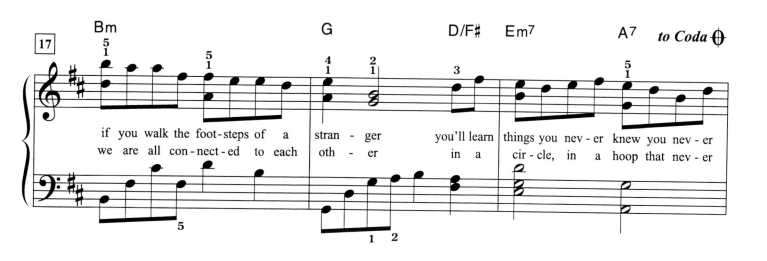

*Chorus:*

knew.  Have you  ev - er heard the wolf cry to the  blue corn  moon,  or

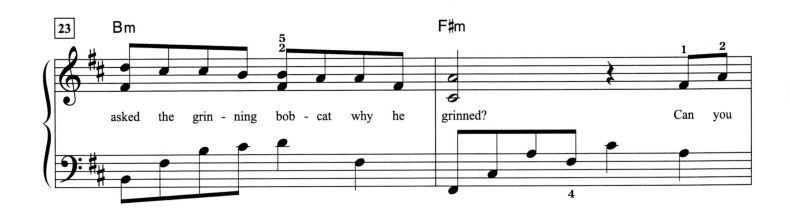

asked  the  grin - ning  bob - cat  why  he  grinned?  Can  you

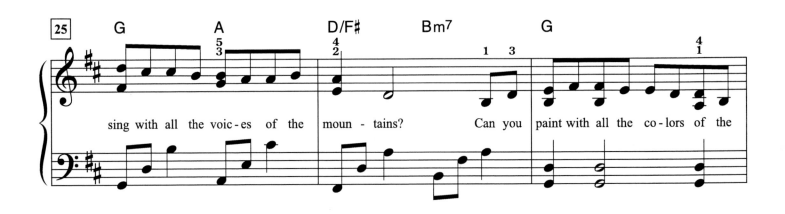

sing  with  all  the  voic - es  of  the  moun - tains?  Can you  paint with all  the  co - lors of the

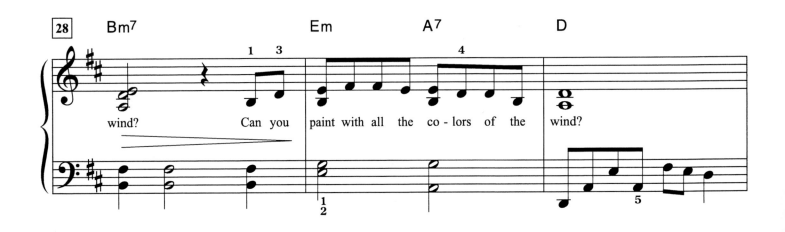

wind?  Can you  paint with all  the  co - lors  of  the  wind?

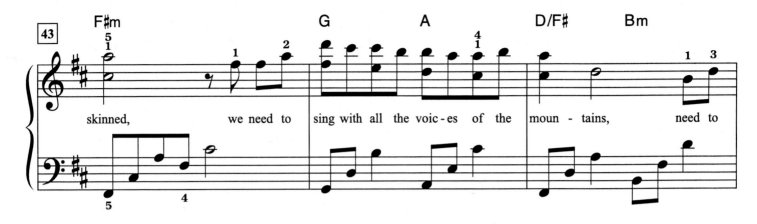

skinned, we need to sing with all the voic-es of the moun-tains, need to

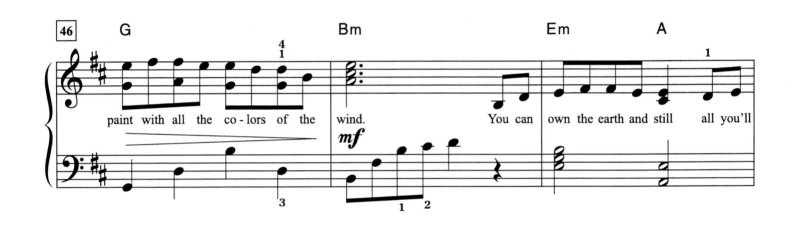

paint with all the co-lors of the wind. You can own the earth and still all you'll

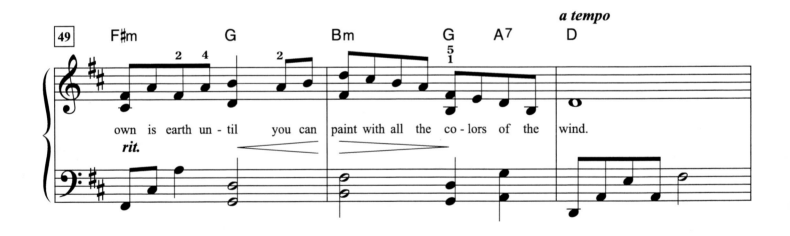

own is earth un-til you can paint with all the co-lors of the wind.

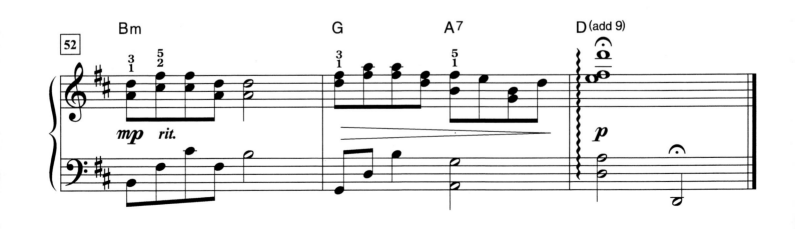

# CONCERNING HOBBITS

*(from The Lord of the Rings: The Fellowship of the Ring)*

By Howard Shore
Arranged by Dan Coates

# CORPSE BRIDE

## (Main Title)

Music by Danny Elfman
Arranged by Dan Coates

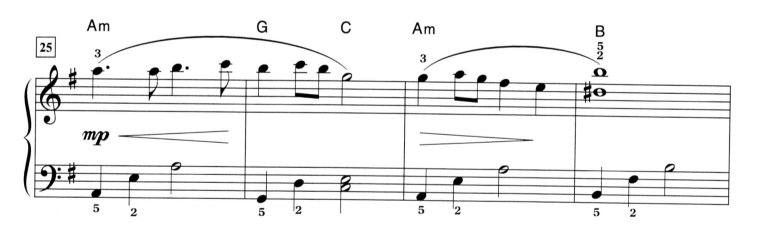

# DANCING QUEEN

## (from *Mamma Mia!*)

**Bright disco beat, in two**

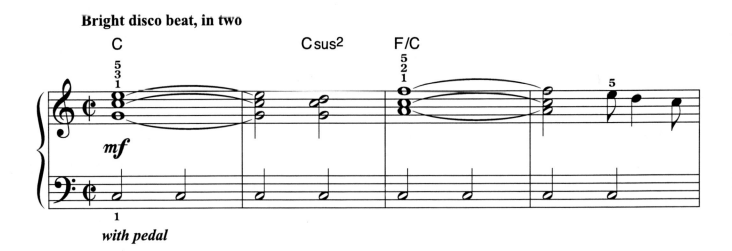

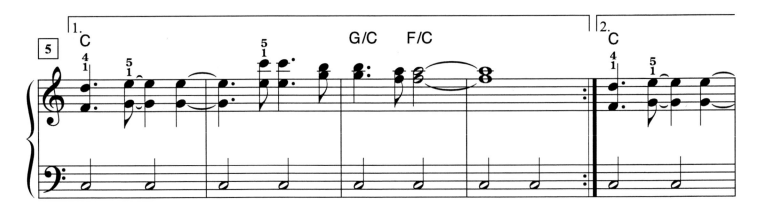

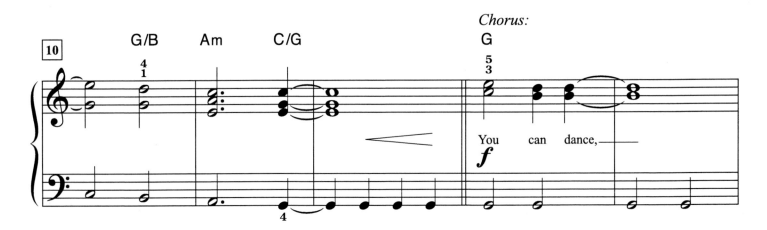

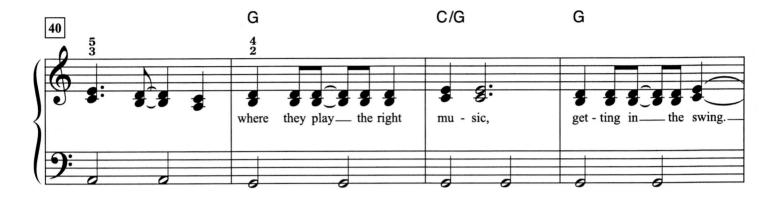

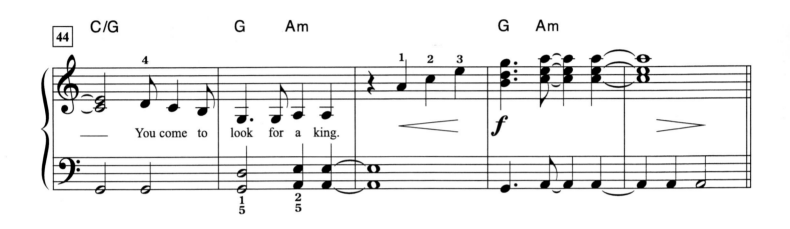

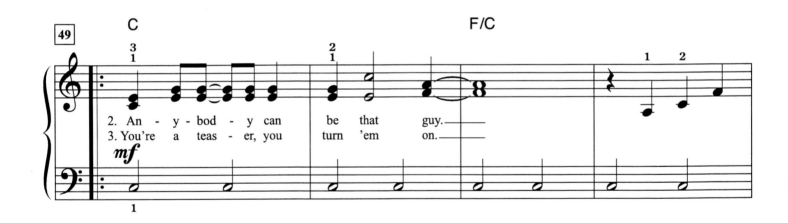

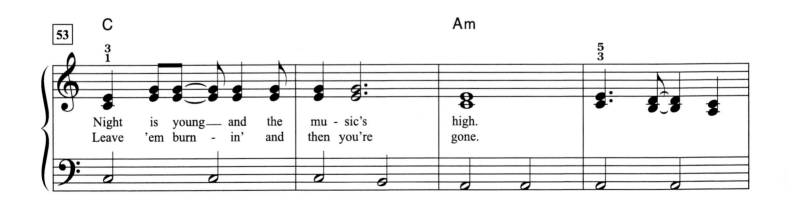

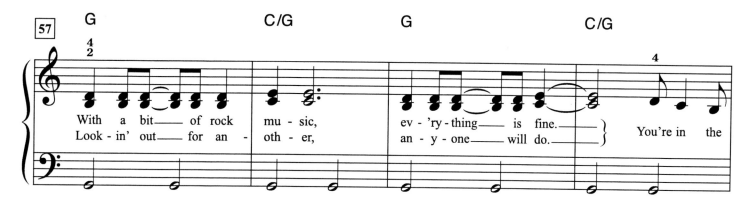

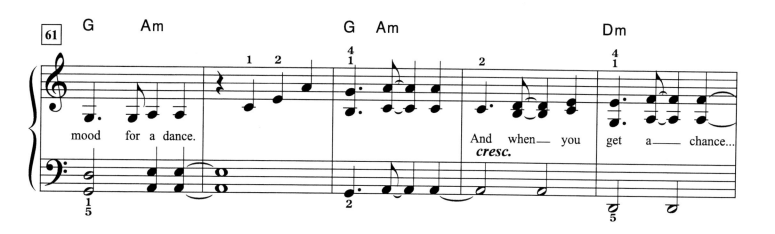

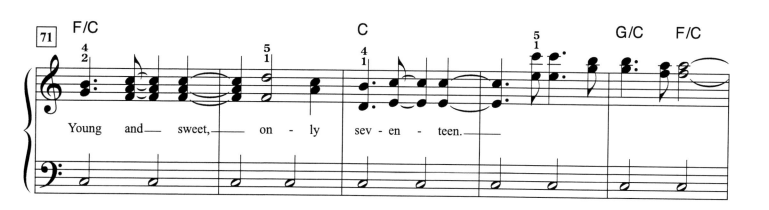

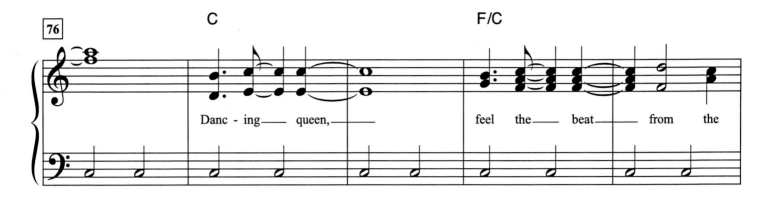

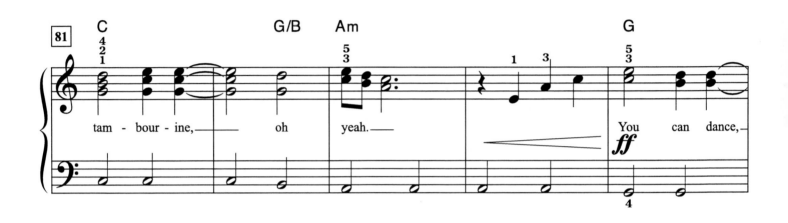

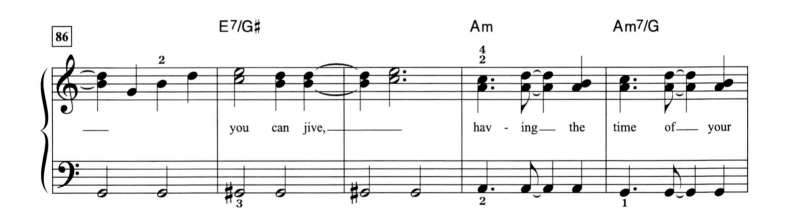

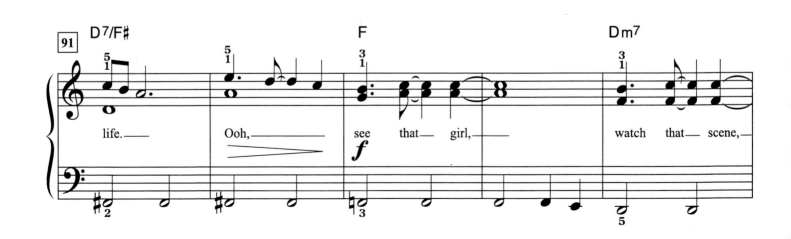

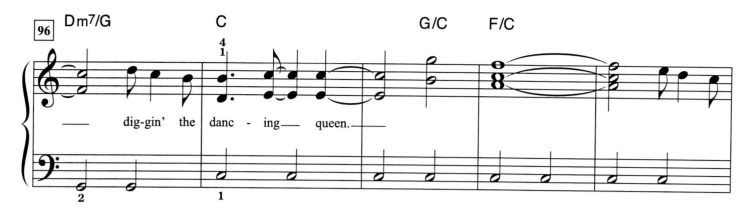

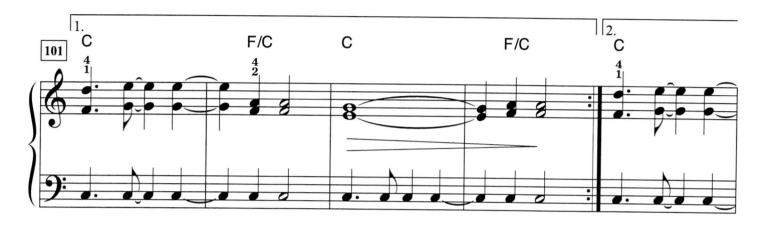

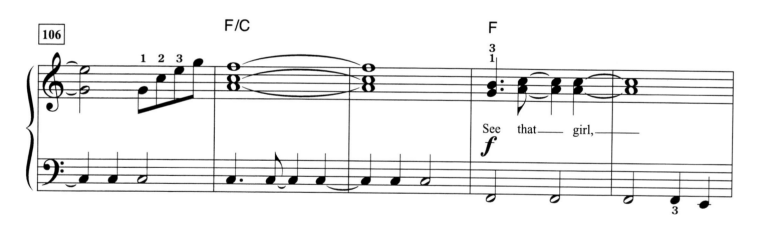

# THE DARK KNIGHT OVERTURE

(from *The Dark Knight*)

Composed by
Hans Zimmer and James Newton Howard
Arranged by Dan Coates

**Mysteriously**

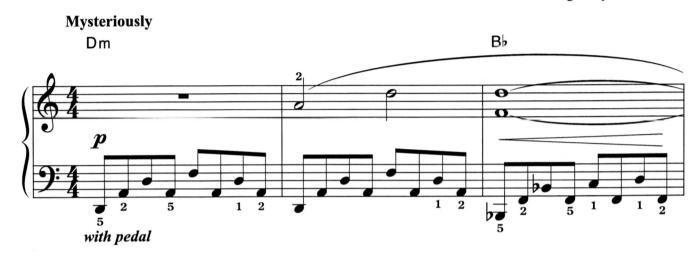

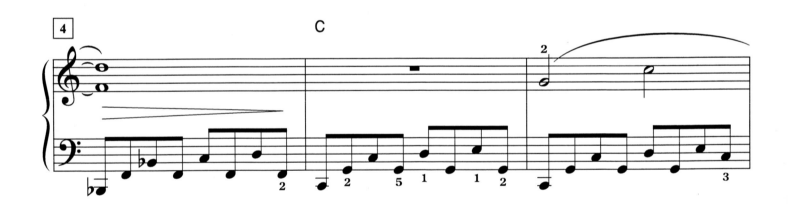

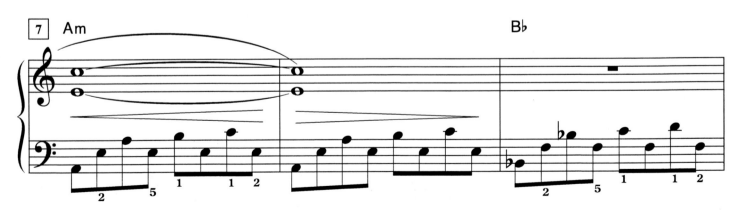

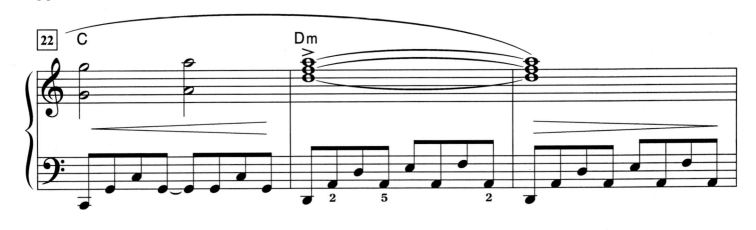

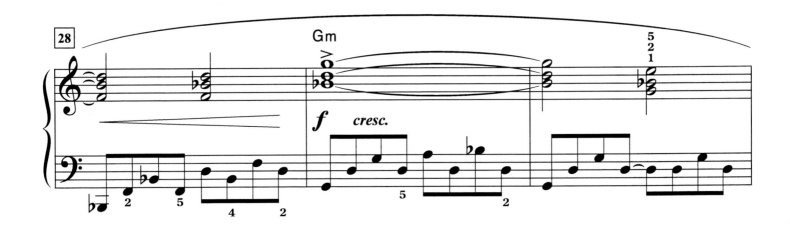

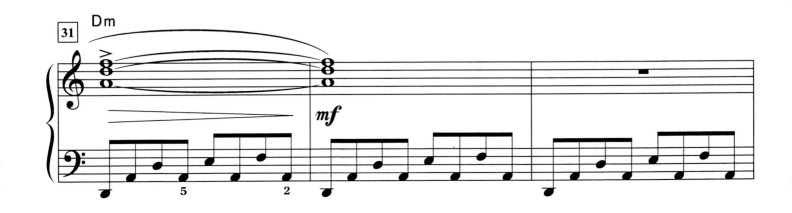

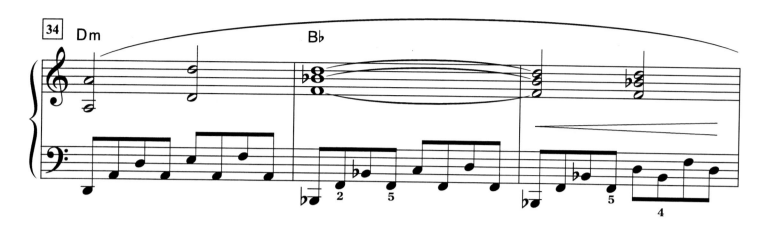

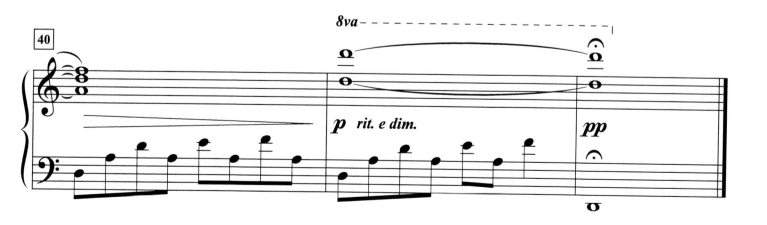

# DISCOMBOBULATE

(from *Sherlock Holmes*)

Composed by Hans Zimmer
Arranged by Dan Coates

41

# DON'T FORGET ME

## (from *SMASH*)

Lyrics by Scott Wittman and Marc Shaiman
Music by Marc Shaiman
Arranged by Dan Coates

and if some - thing good___ can come from bad,___ the

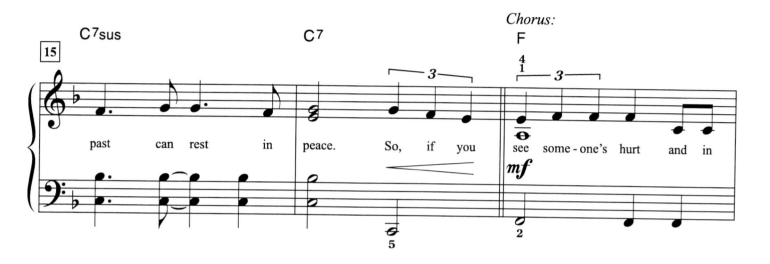

past can rest in peace. So, if you see some - one's hurt and in

need of a hand, don't for - get___ me.___ Or hear a

mel - o - dy cry - ing from some ba - by grand, well, don't for - get___ me.___

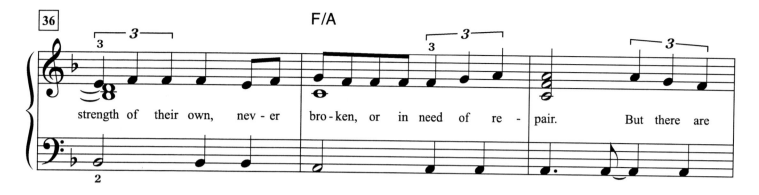

strength of their own, nev - er bro - ken, or in need of re - pair. But there are

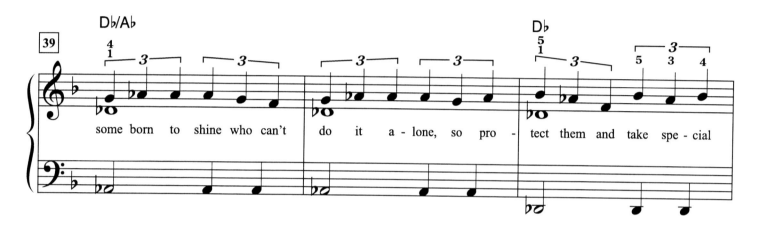

some born to shine who can't do it a - lone, so pro - tect them and take spe - cial

care. Take care.

And don't for - get____ me.

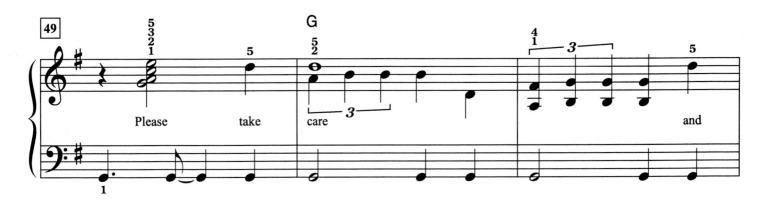

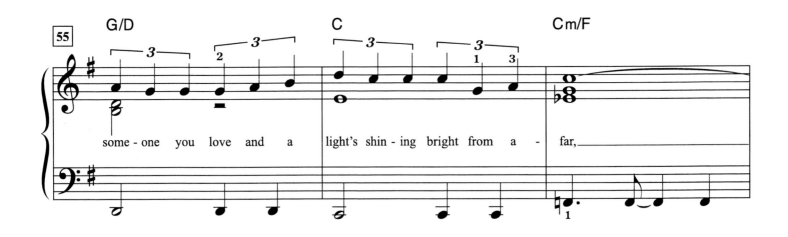

of - fer a prayer, _____ and please _____ let me

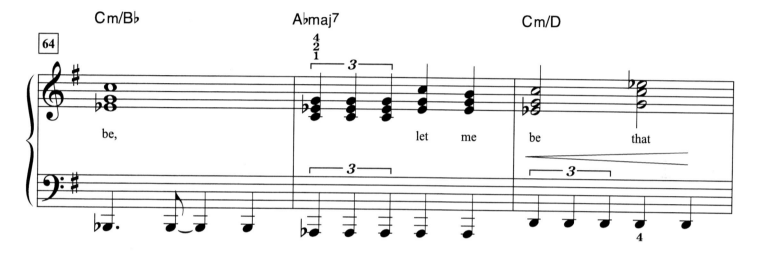

be, let me be that

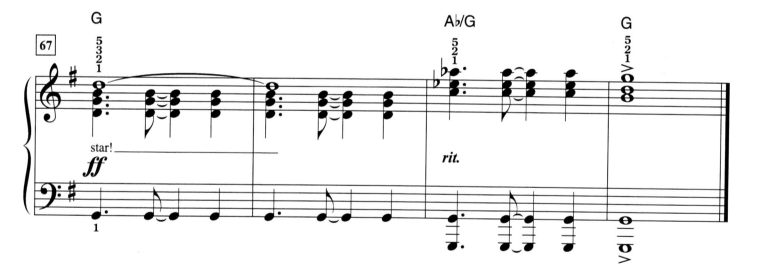

star! _____

*ff*

*rit.*

*Verse 2:*
But forget every man who I ever met
'Cause they all only lived to control.
For a kiss they paid a thousand,
Yet they paid fifty cents for my soul.
They took their piece, the price of fame
That no one can repay.
Ah, but they didn't buy me when they bought my name
And that is why I pray.
So, if you...
*(To Chorus:)*

# DON'T RAIN ON MY PARADE

(from *Funny Girl, Glee* Cast)

Words by Bob Merrill
Music by Jule Styne
Arranged by Dan Coates

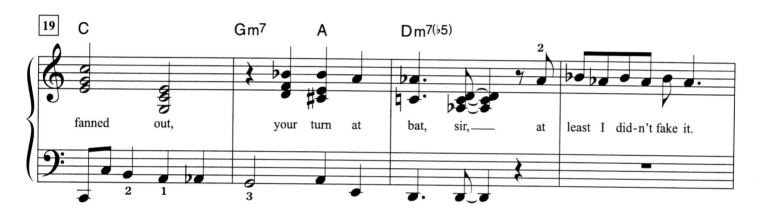

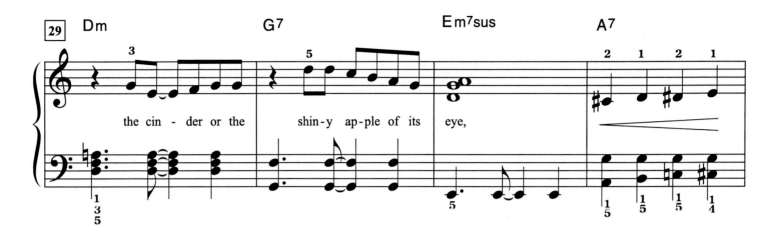

**29** Dm · G7 · Em7sus · A7

the cin - der or the shin-y ap-ple of its eye,

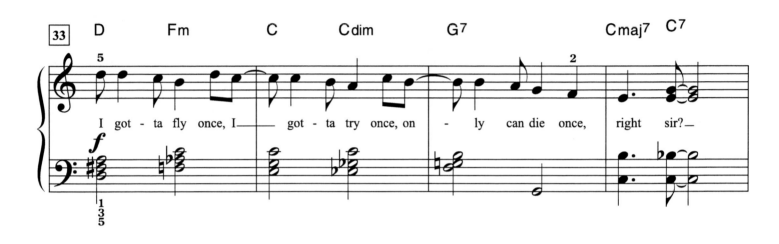

**33** D · Fm · C · Cdim · G7 · Cmaj7 C7

I got - ta fly once, I——— got - ta try once, on - ly can die once, right sir?—

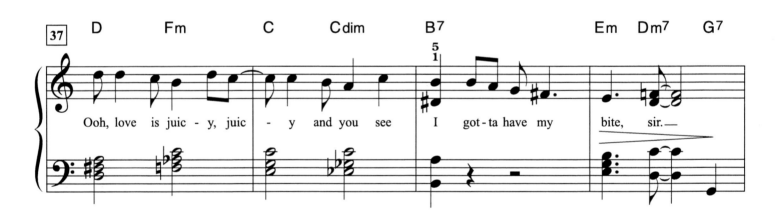

**37** D · Fm · C · Cdim · B7 · Em Dm7 G7

Ooh, love is juic - y, juic - y and you see I got - ta have my bite, sir.—

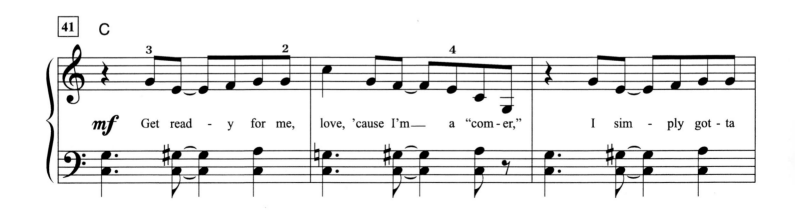

**41** C

Get read - y for me, love, 'cause I'm— a "com - er," I sim - ply got - ta

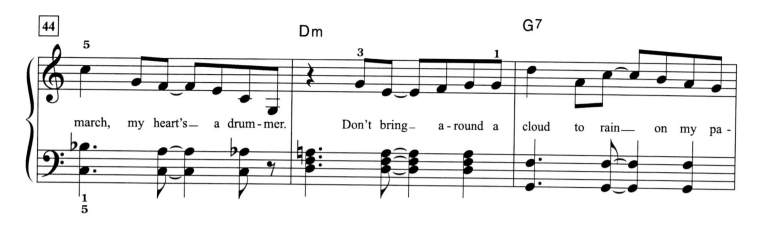

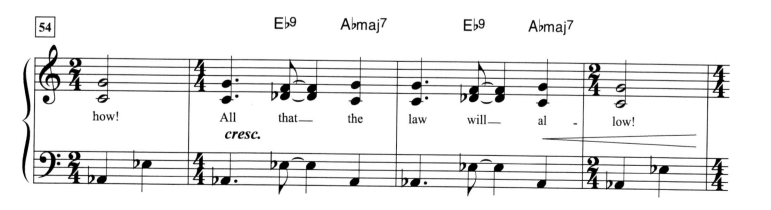

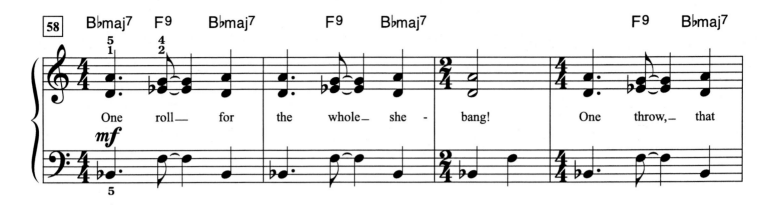

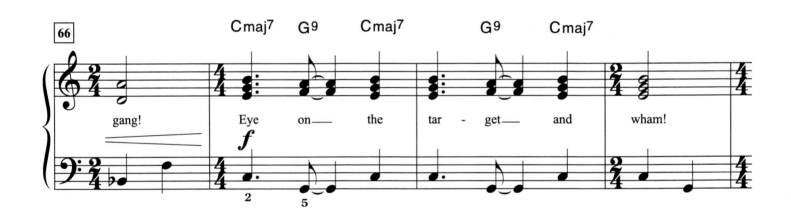

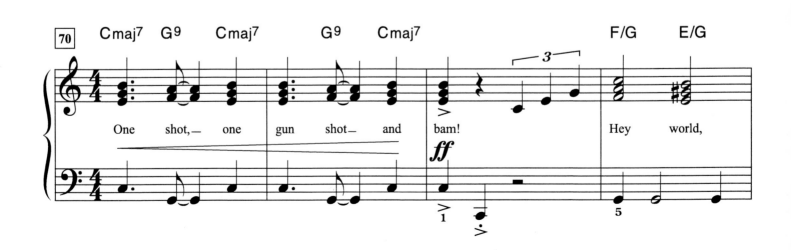

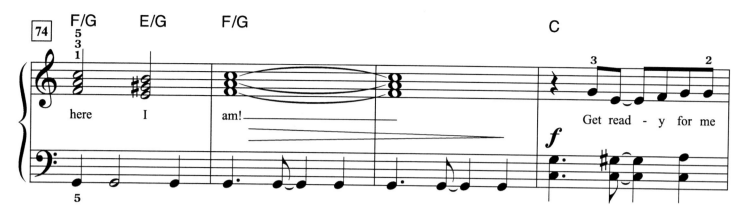

here I am! Get read - y for me

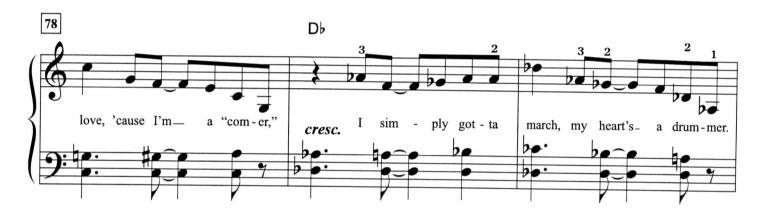

love, 'cause I'm— a "com - er," I sim - ply got - ta march, my heart's— a drum - mer.

cresc.

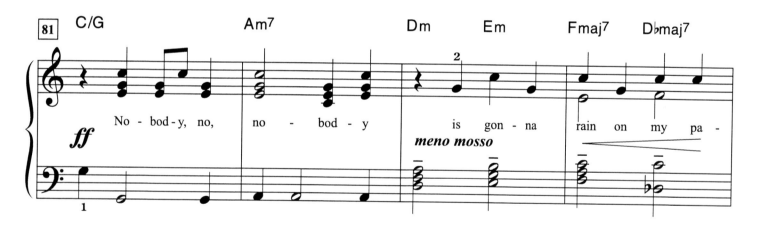

No - bod - y, no, no - bod - y is gon - na rain on my pa -

meno mosso

ff

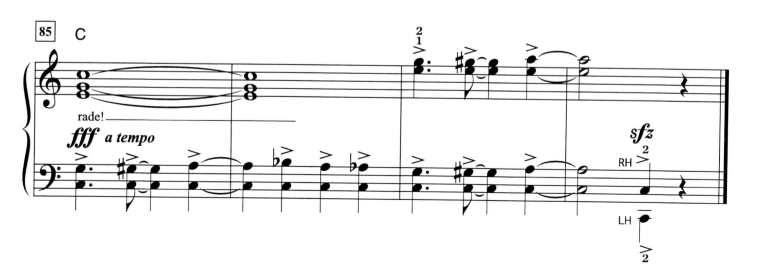

rade!

fff a tempo

# DREAM IS COLLAPSING

(from *Inception*)

Composed by Hans Zimmer
Arranged by Dan Coates

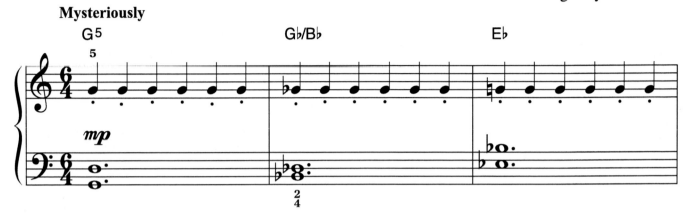

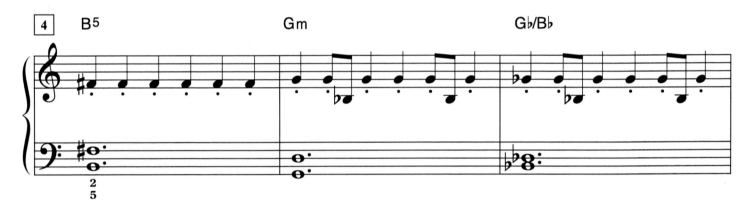

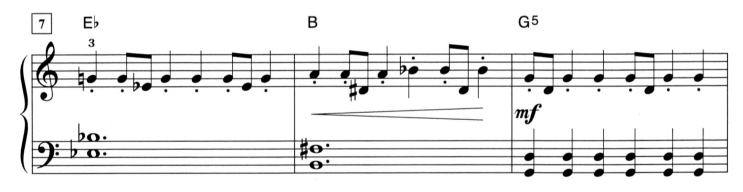

# DON'T STOP BELIEVIN'

(from *Rock of Ages*)

Words and Music by
Jonathan Cain, Neal Schon and Steve Perry
Arranged by Dan Coates

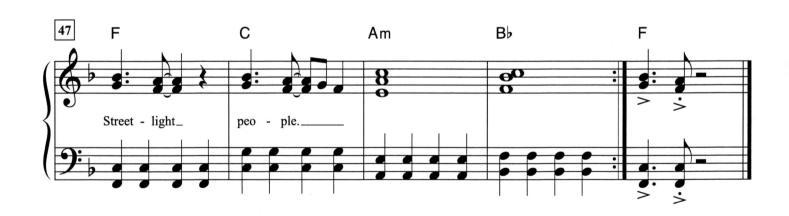

Verse 3:
A singer in a smoky room,
The smell of wine and cheap perfume.
For a smile they can share the night
It goes on and on and on and on.

Verse 4:
Working hard to get my fill.
Everybody wants a thrill,
Payin' anything to roll the dice
Just one more time.

Verse 5:
Some will win and some will lose,
Some were born to sing the blues.
Oh, the movie never ends,
It goes on and on and on and on.

# FALLING SLOWLY

## (from *Once*)

Words and Music by
Glen Hansard and Marketa Irglova
Arranged by Dan Coates

**Slowly, with expression**

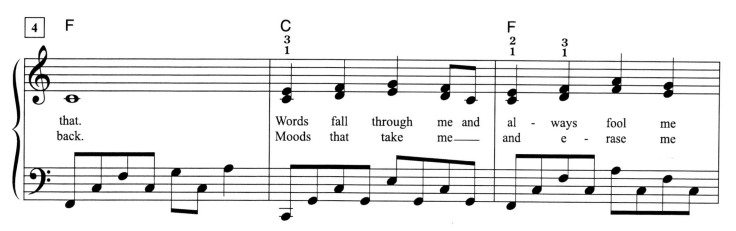

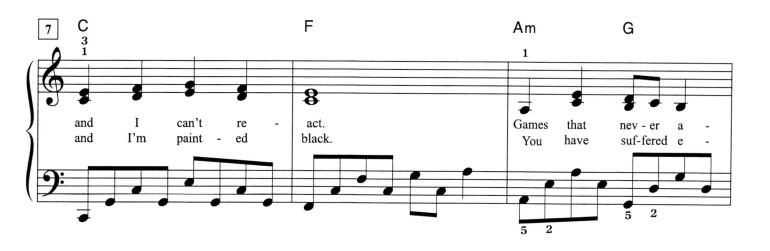

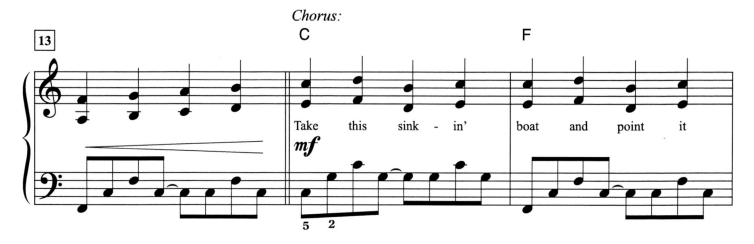

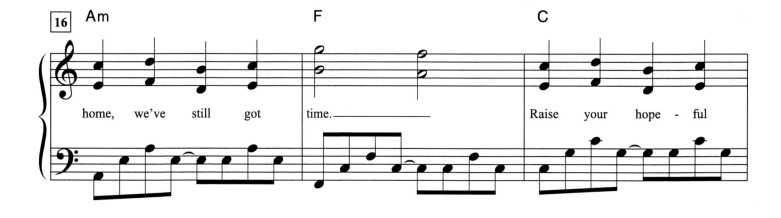

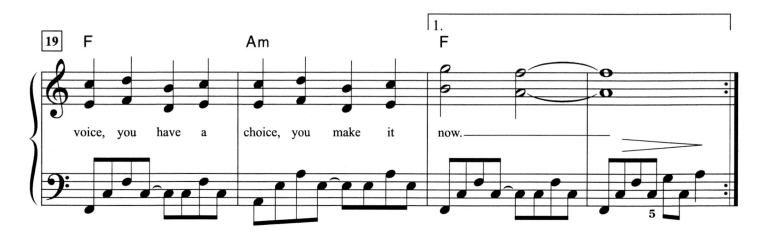

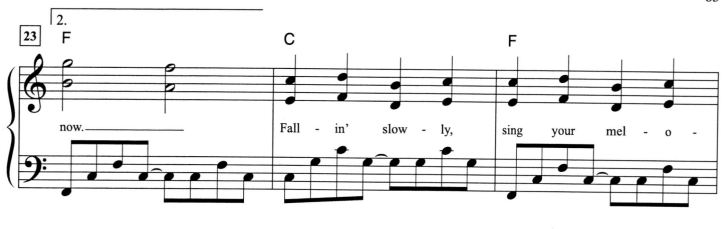

now._____ Fall - in' slow - ly, sing your mel - o -

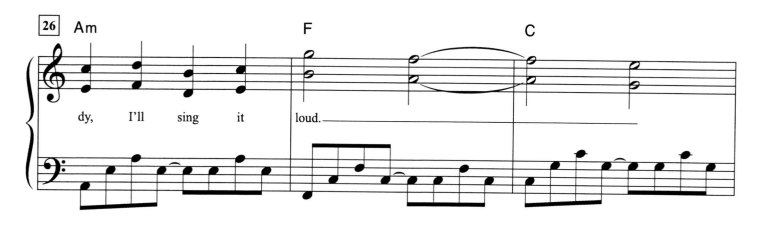

dy, I'll sing it loud._____

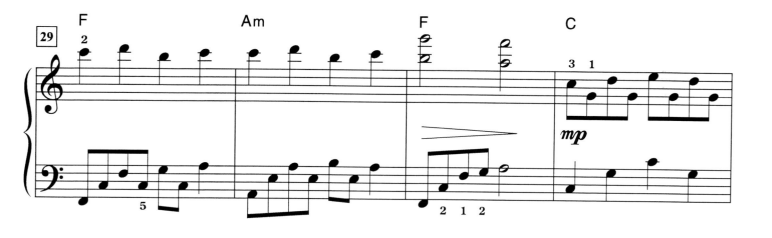

dim.    p    rit. e dim.    pp

# HARRY'S WONDROUS WORLD

(from *Harry Potter and The Sorcerer's Stone*)

By John Williams
Arranged by Dan Coates

# HEDWIG'S THEME

(from *Harry Potter and the Sorcerer's Stone*)

By John Williams
Arranged by Dan Coates

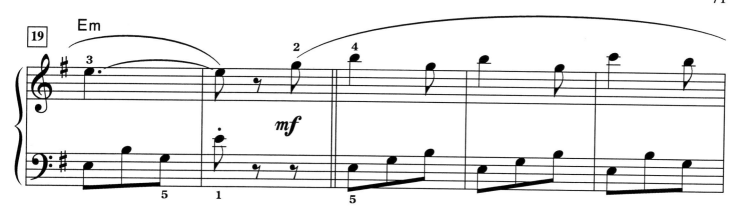

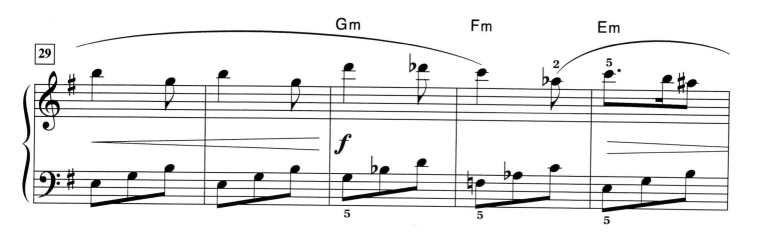

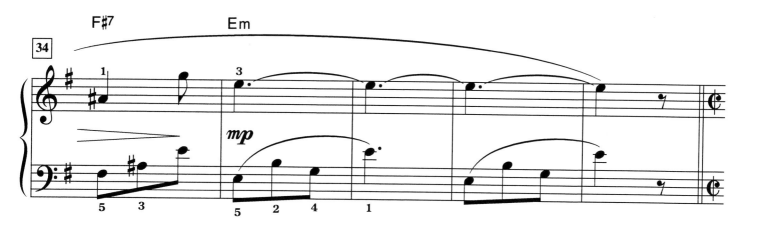

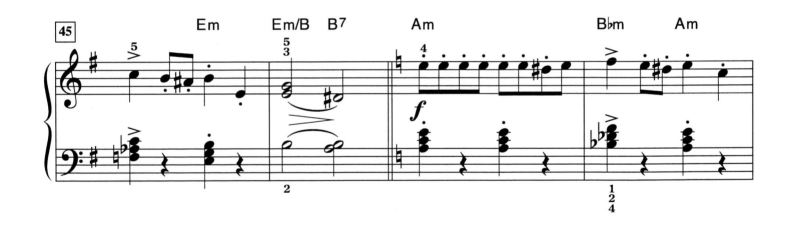

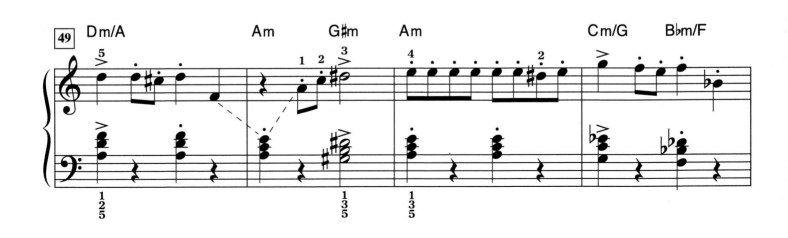

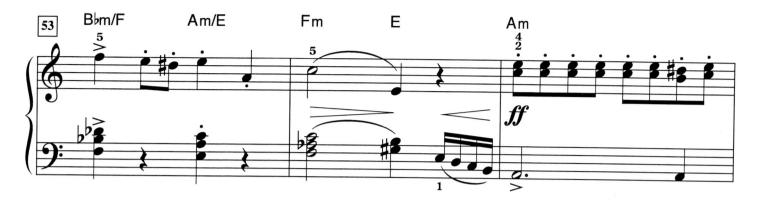

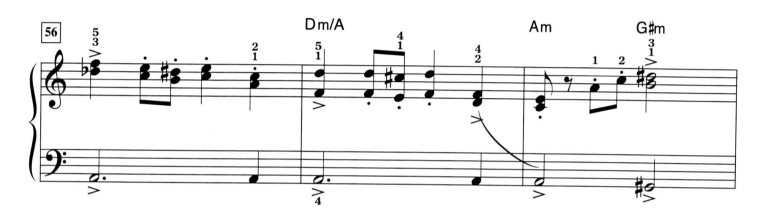

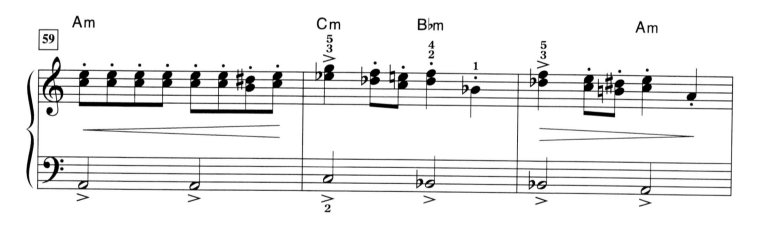

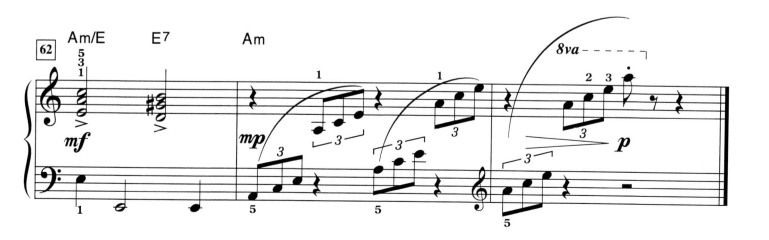

# I DON'T WANT TO MISS A THING

(from *Armageddon*)

Words and Music by Diane Warren<br/>Arranged by Dan Coates

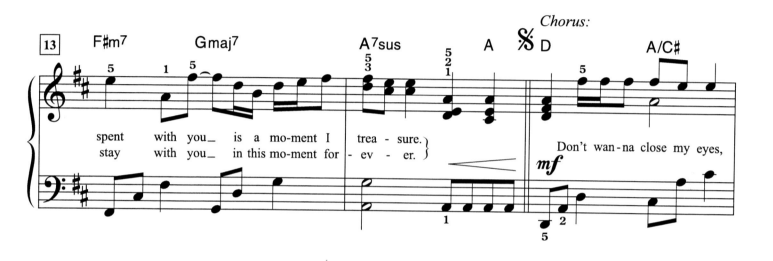

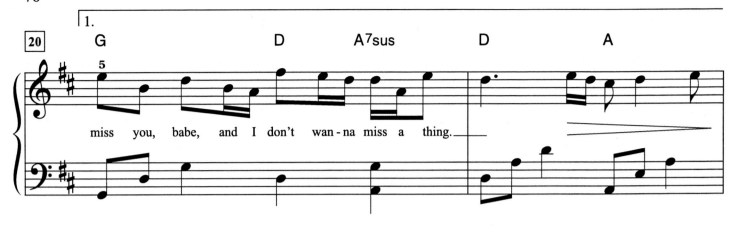

*Bridge:*

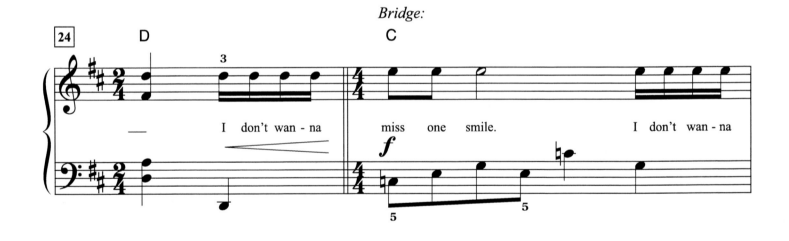

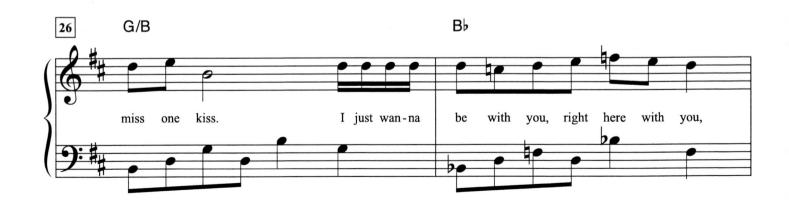

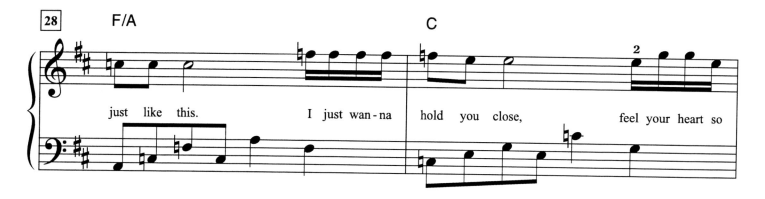

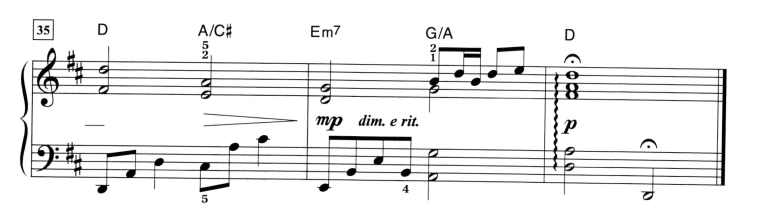

# I COULD HAVE DANCED ALL NIGHT

(from *My Fair Lady*)

Lyrics by Alan Jay Lerner
Music by Frederick Loewe
Arranged by Dan Coates

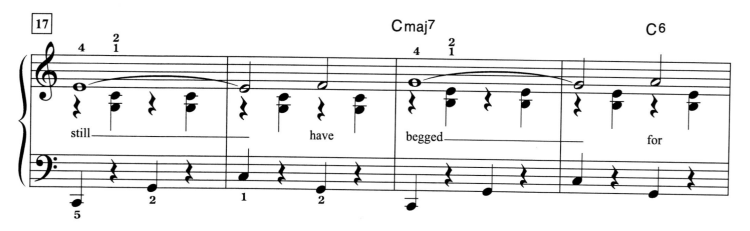

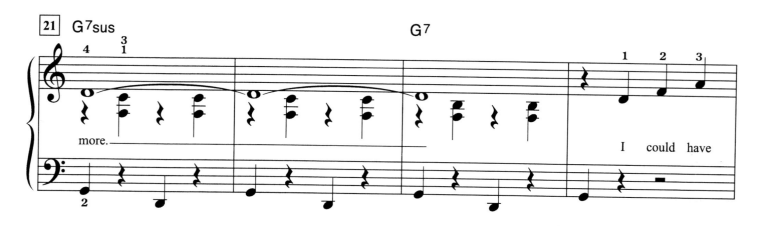

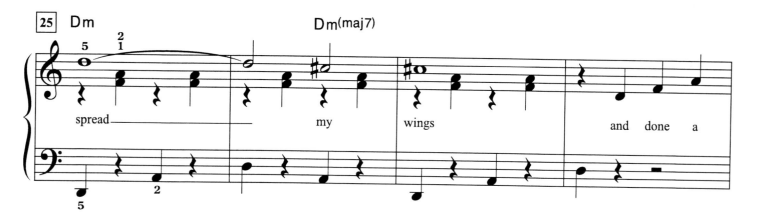

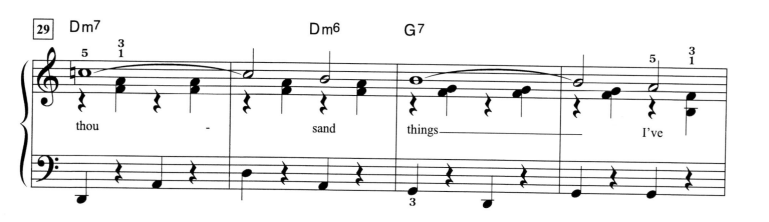

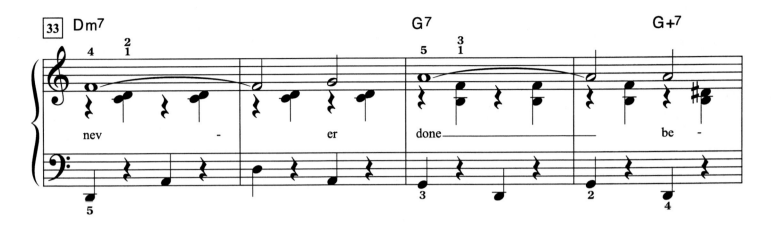

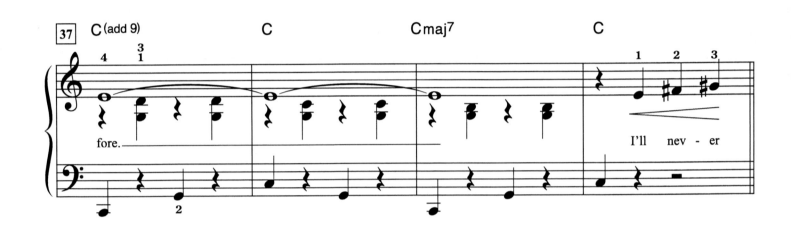

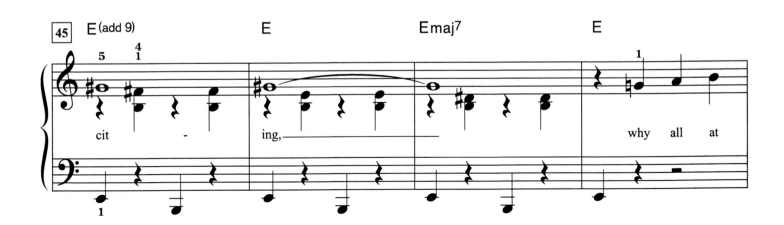

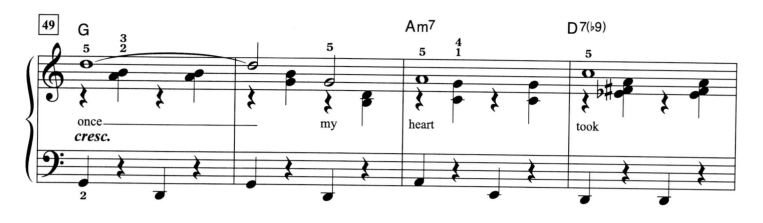

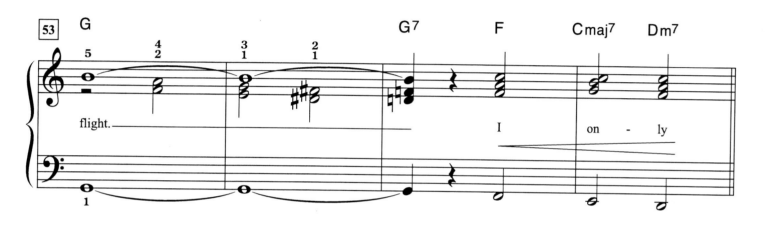

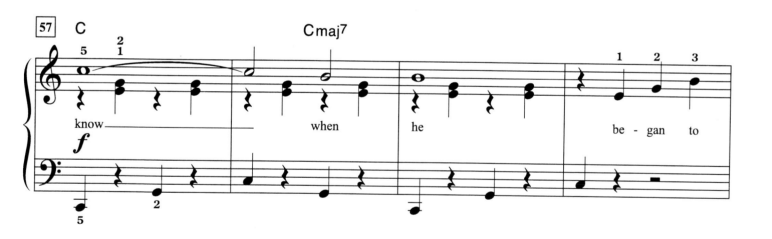

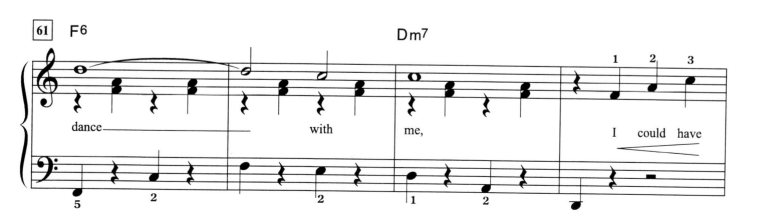

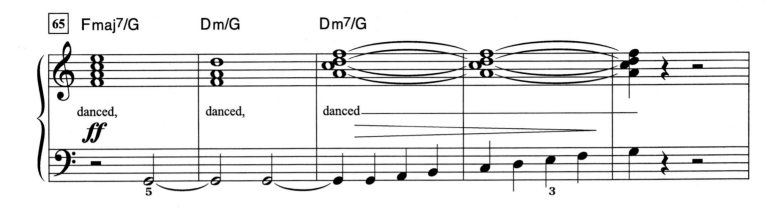

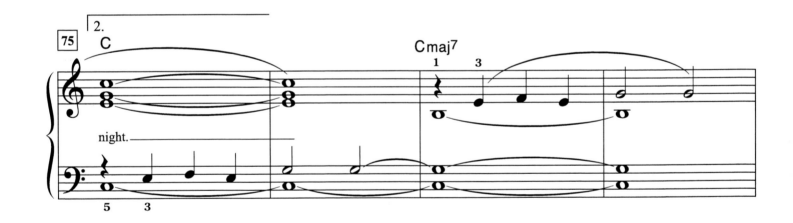

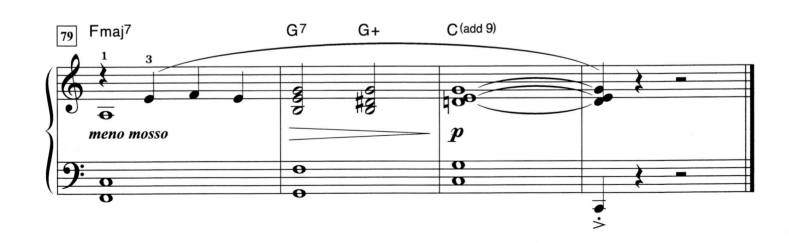

# I HAVE NOTHING

## (from *The Bodyguard*)

Words and Music by
Linda Thompson and David Foster
Arranged by Dan Coates

84

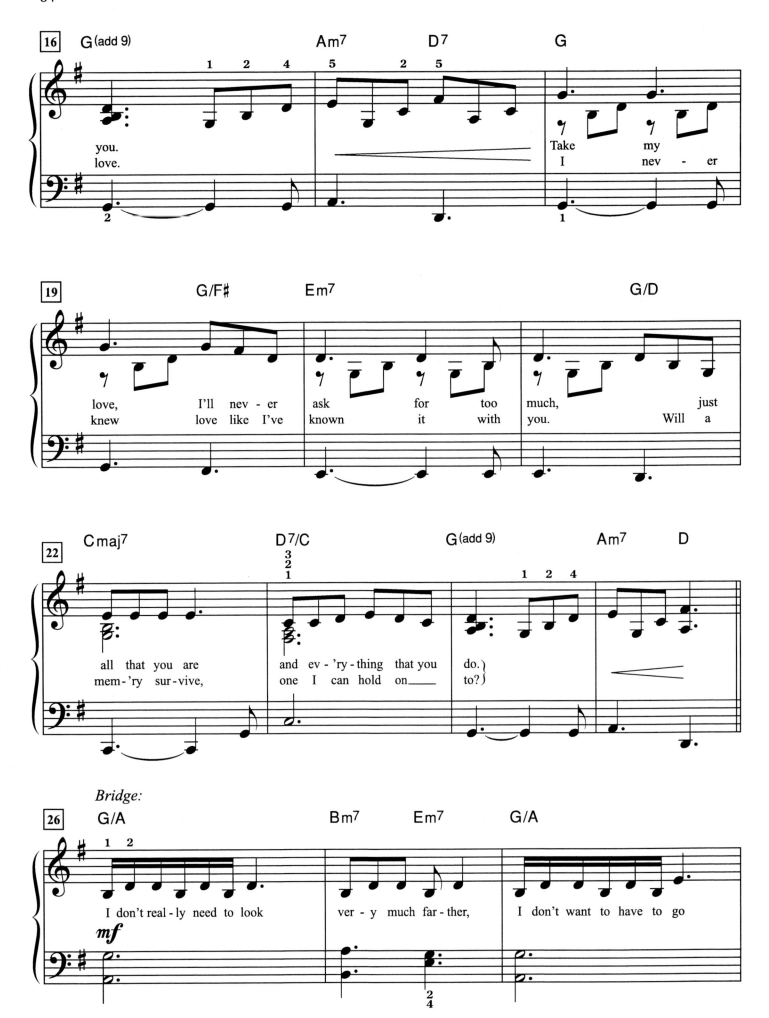

where you don't fol - low. I won't hold it back a - gain, this pas - sion in - side. Can't

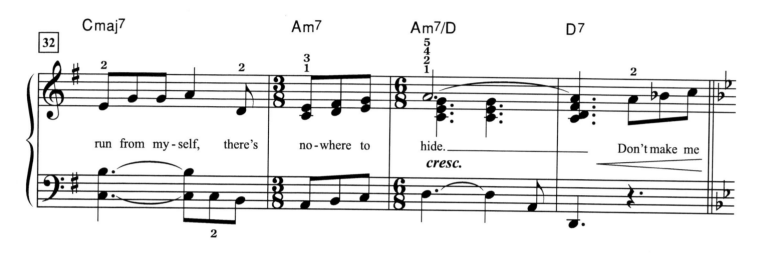

run from my - self, there's no - where to hide. *cresc.* Don't make me

*Chorus:*

close_____ one more door, I don't want to hurt_____ an - y - more. Stay in my

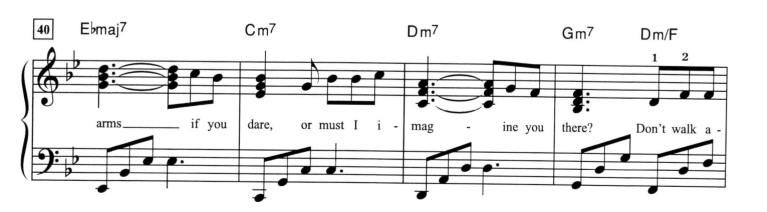

arms_____ if you dare, or must I i - mag - ine you there? Don't walk a -

Coda

Dm7 Gm7 Cm7 Dm7 Gm7

Don't walk a - way from me._____ Don't you dare walk a -

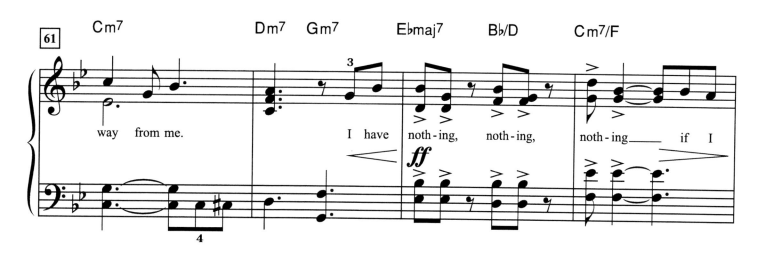

Cm7 Dm7 Gm7 Ebmaj7 Bb/D Cm7/F

way from me. I have noth - ing, noth - ing, noth - ing_____ if I

ff

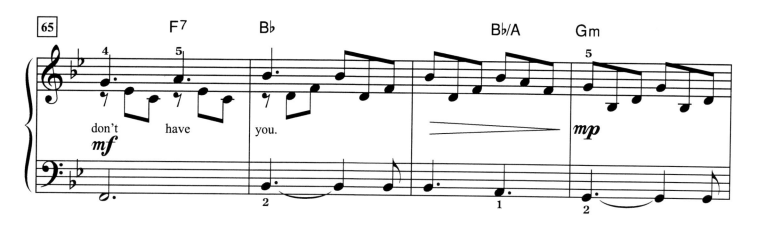

F7 Bb Bb/A Gm

don't have you.

mf mp

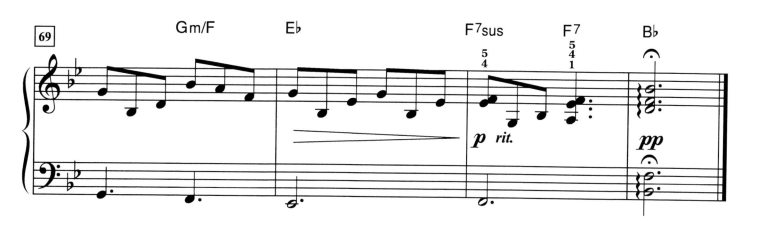

Gm/F Eb F7sus F7 Bb

p rit. pp

# I'LL BE THERE FOR YOU

## (Theme from *Friends*)

Words by David Crane, Marta Kauffman,
Allee Willis, Phil Solem and Danny Wilde
Music by Michael Skloff
Arranged by Dan Coates

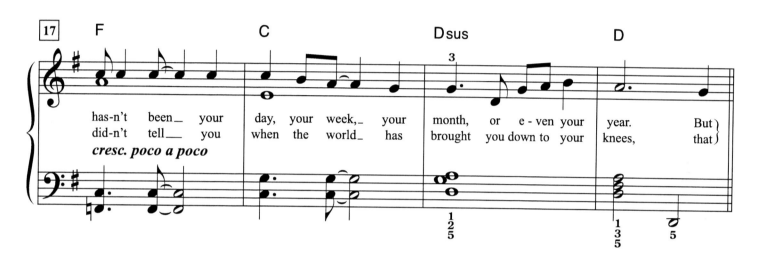

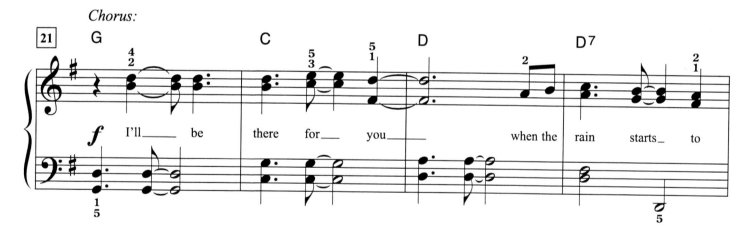

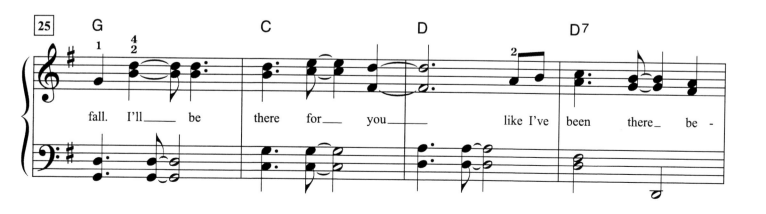

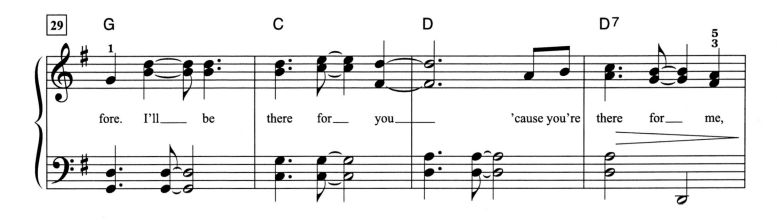

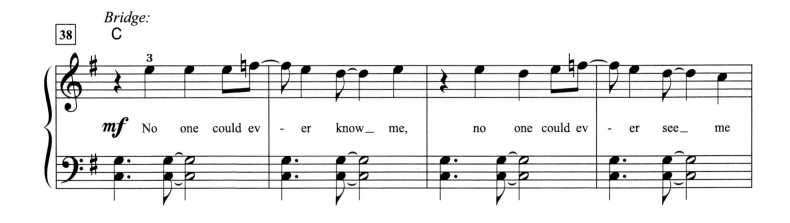

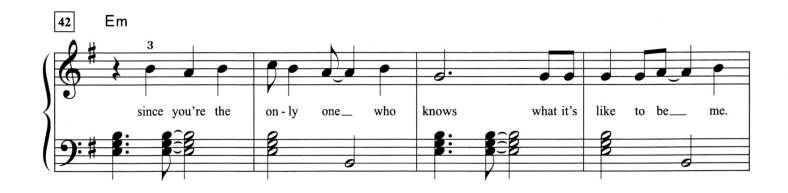

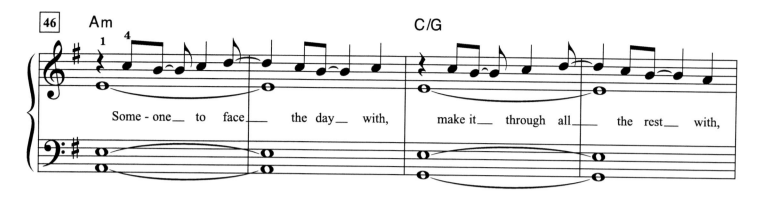

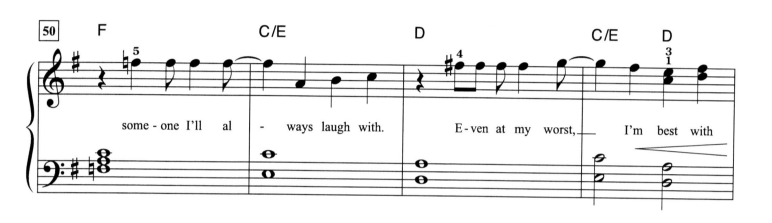

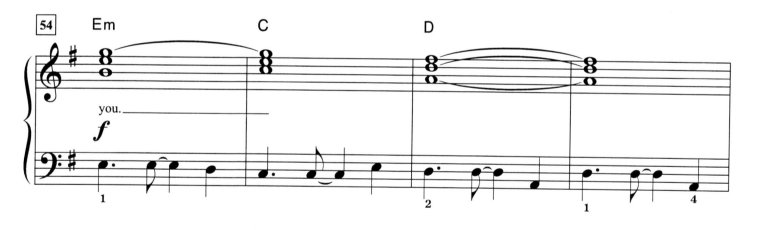

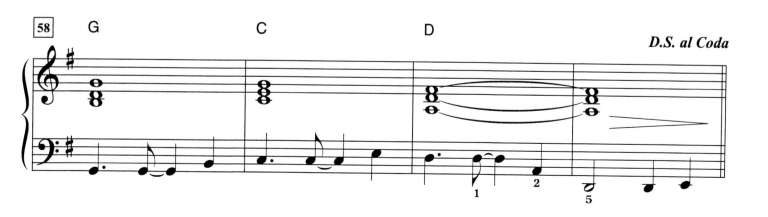

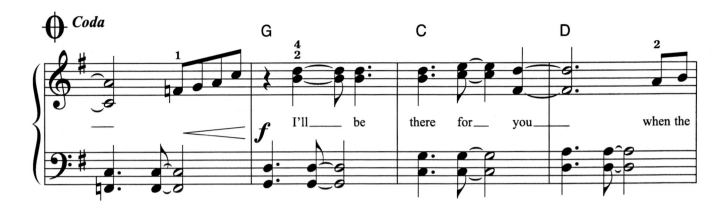

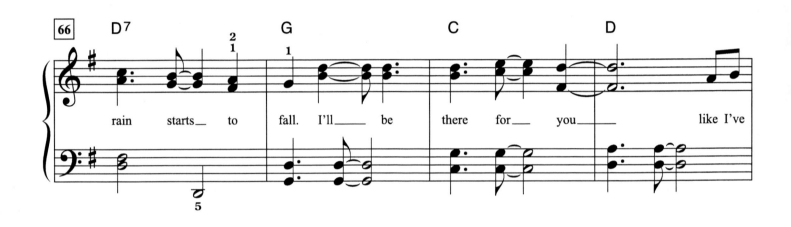

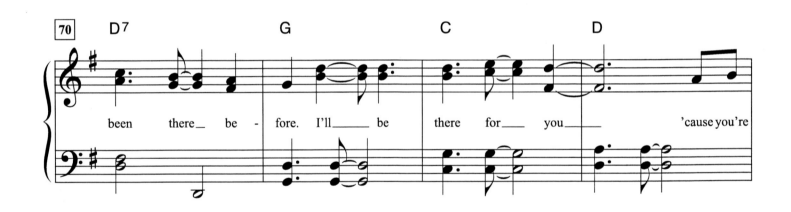

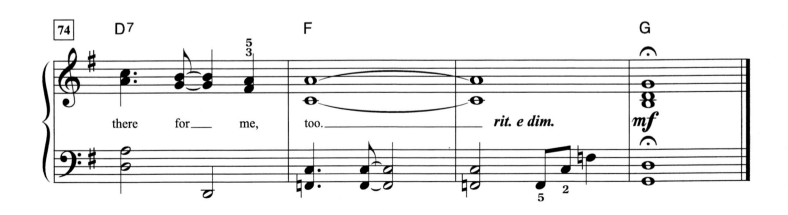

# IT WILL RAIN

(from *The Twilight Saga: Breaking Dawn Part 1*)

Words and Music by
Bruno Mars,
Philip Lawrence and Ari Levine
Arranged by Dan Coates

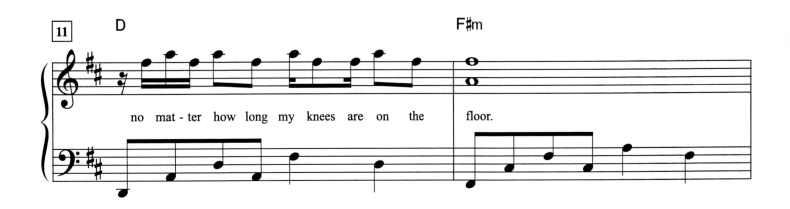

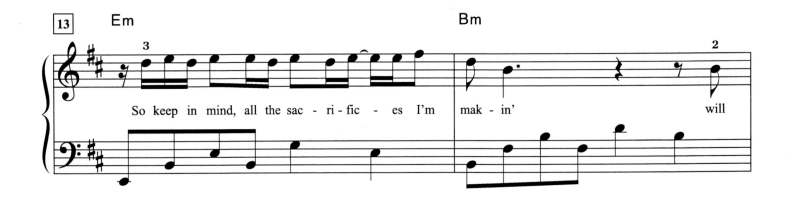

*Verse 2:*
I'll never be your mother's favorite,
Your daddy can't even look me in the eye.
If I was in their shoes, I'd be doin' the same thing.
Sayin', "There goes my little girl walkin' with that troublesome guy."
But they're just afraid of something they can't understand,
But little darling, watch me change their minds.
Yeah, for you, I'll try, I'll try, I'll try, I'll try.
I'll pick up these broken pieces 'til I'm bleeding,
If that'll make you mine.
*(To Chorus:)*

# THE IMPERIAL MARCH
# (DARTH VADER'S THEME)

(from *Star Wars: The Empire Strikes Back*)

Music by John Williams
Arranged by Dan Coates

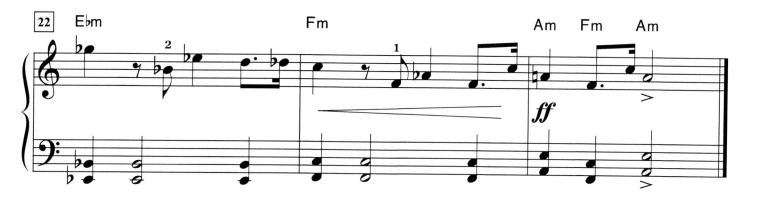

# INTO THE WEST

(from *The Lord of the Rings: The Return of the King*)

Words and Music by
Howard Shore, Fran Walsh and Annie Lennox
Arranged by Dan Coates

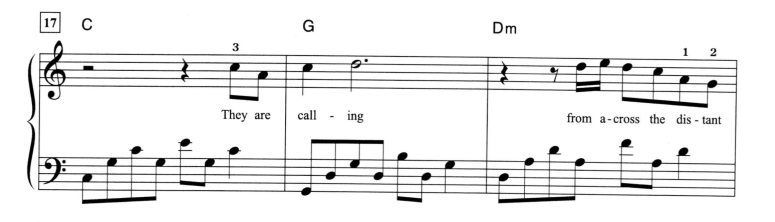

all of your fears ____ will pass a - way.

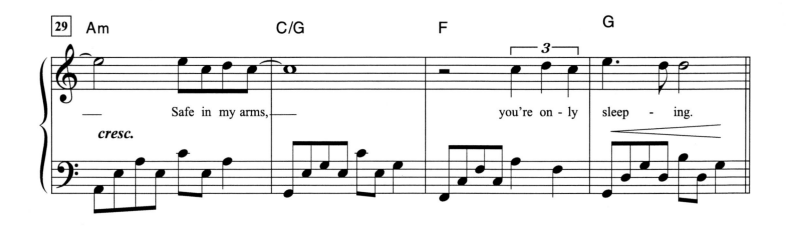

Safe in my arms, ____ you're on - ly sleep - ing.

*cresc.*

*Chorus:*

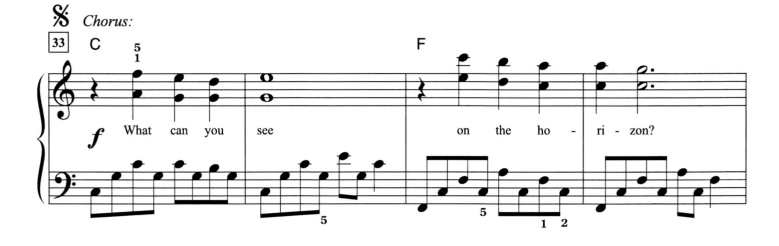

What can you see on the ho - ri - zon?

*f*

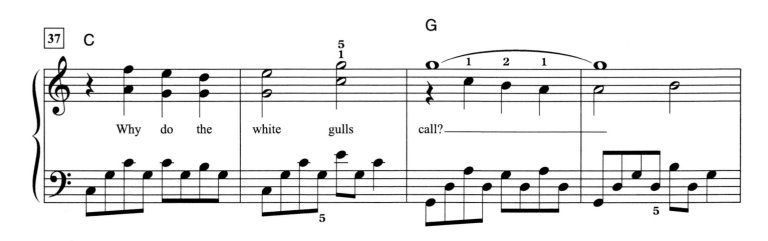

Why do the white gulls call? ____

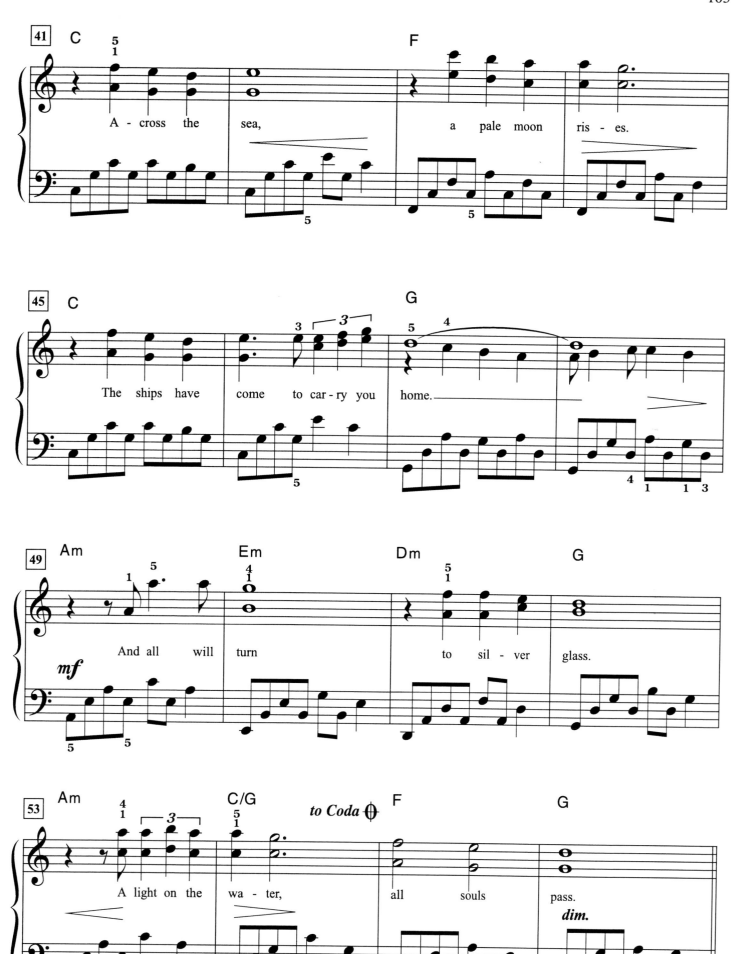

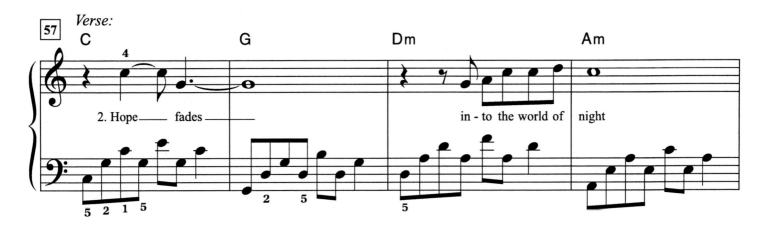

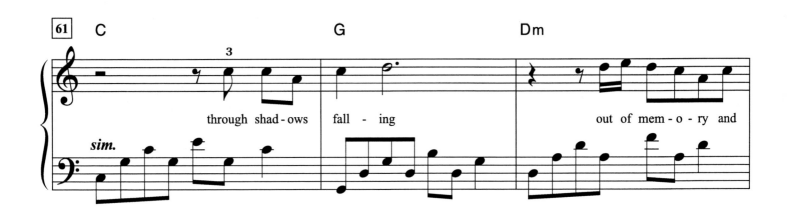

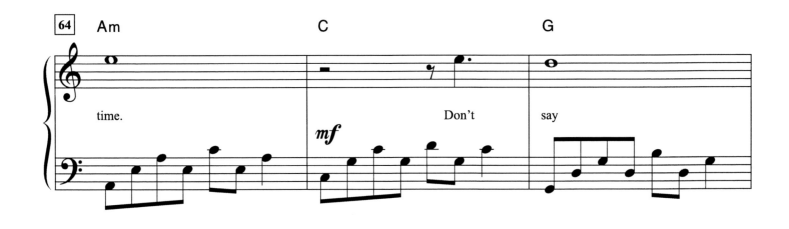

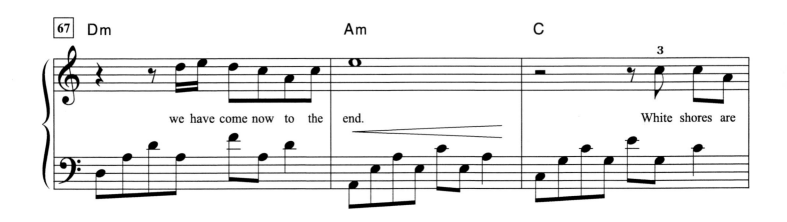

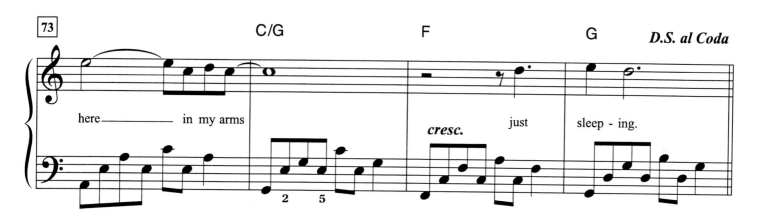

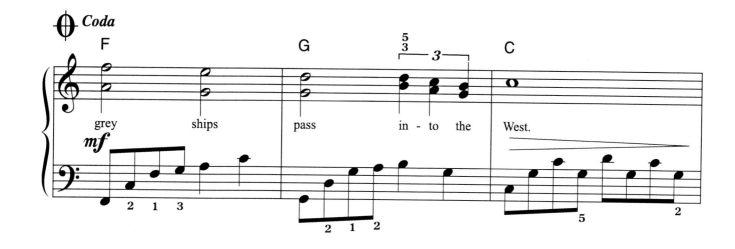

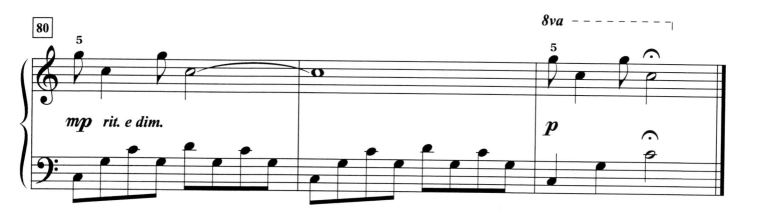

# JAMES BOND THEME

## (from *Dr. No*)

By Monty Norman
Arranged by Dan Coates

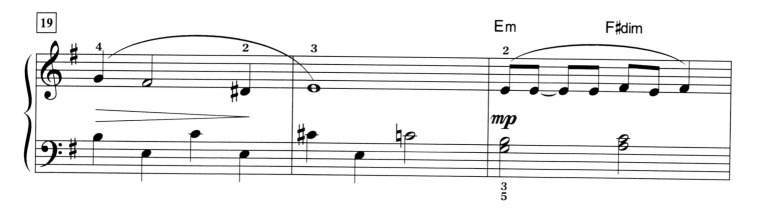

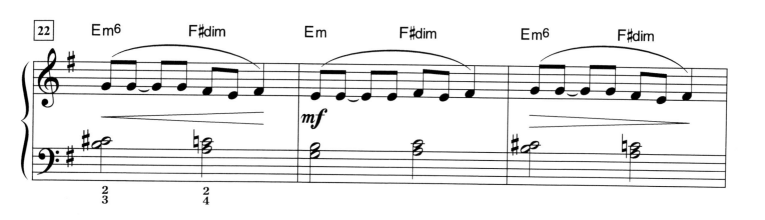

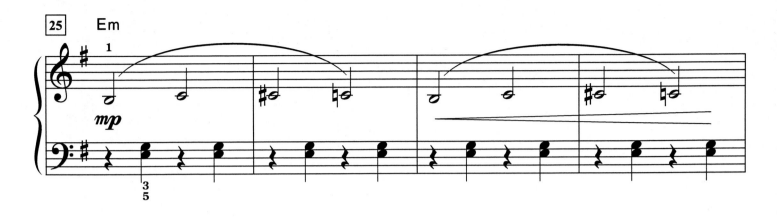

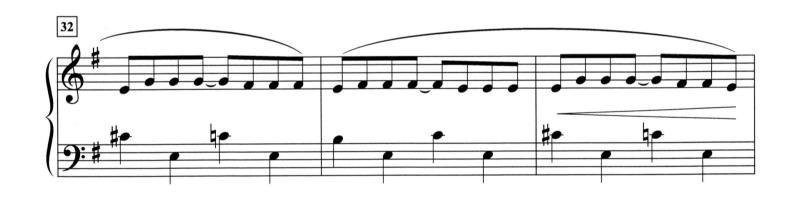

# LET ME BE YOUR STAR

(from *SMASH*)

Lyrics by Scott Wittman and Marc Shaiman
Music by Marc Shaiman
Arranged by Dan Coates

**Moderately bright**

with pedal

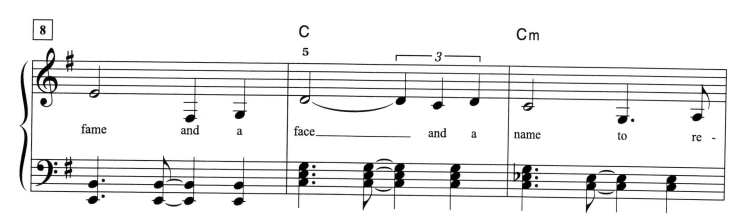

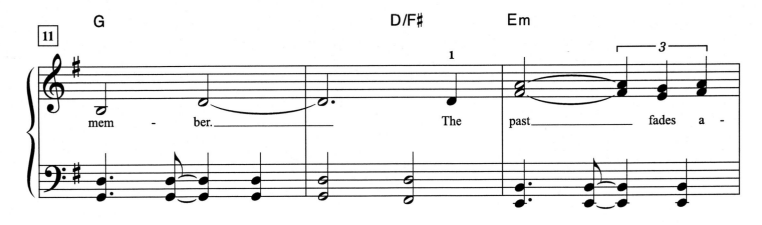

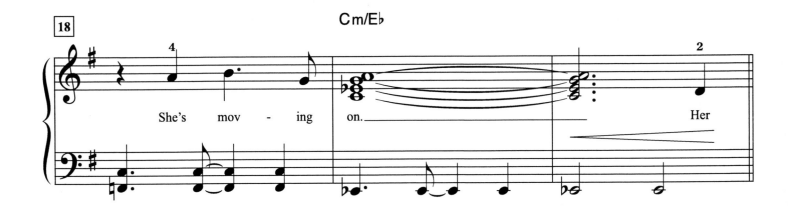

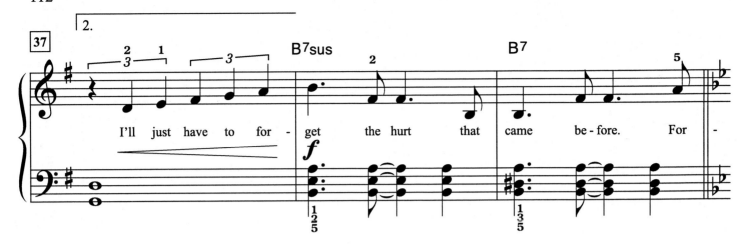

I'll just have to for-get the hurt that came be-fore. For-

get what___ used to be. The past is on the

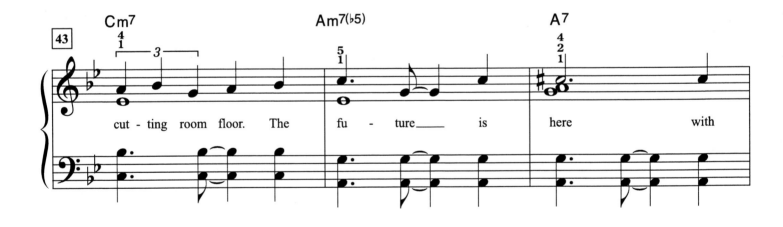

cut-ting room floor. The fu-ture___ is here with

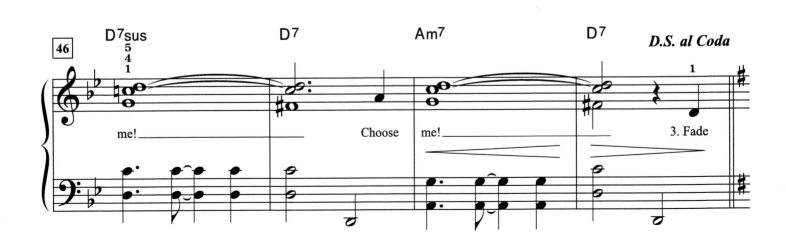

me!___ Choose me!___ 3. Fade

let me be your star.

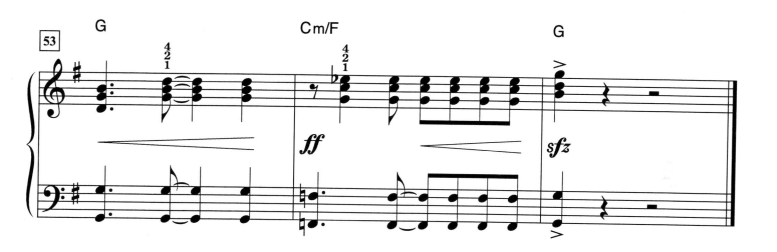

*Verse 2:*

Flash back to a girl with a song in her heart
As she's waiting to start the adventure.
The fire and drive that make dreams come alive,
They fill her soul. She's in control.
The drama, the laughter, the tears just like pearls,
Well, they're all in this girl's repertoire.
It's all for the taking and it's magic we'll be making,
Let me be your star.

*Verse 3:*

Fade up on a star with it all in her sights,
All the love and the lights that surround her.
Someday she'll think twice of the dues and the price
She'll have to pay, but not today!
She'll do all she can for the love of one man
And for millions who love from afar.
I'm what you've been needing, it's all here and her heart's pleading,
Let me be your star.

# LILY'S THEME

## (Main Theme from *Harry Potter and the Deathly Hallows, Part 2*)

By Alexandre Desplat
Arranged by Dan Coates

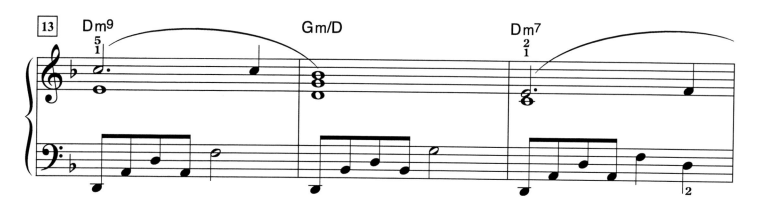

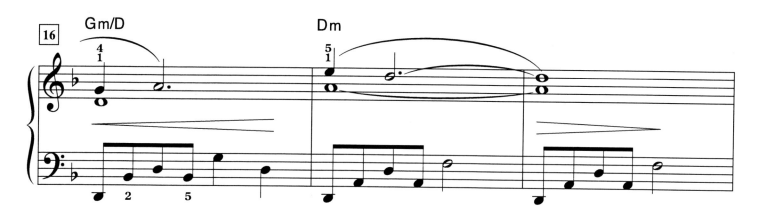

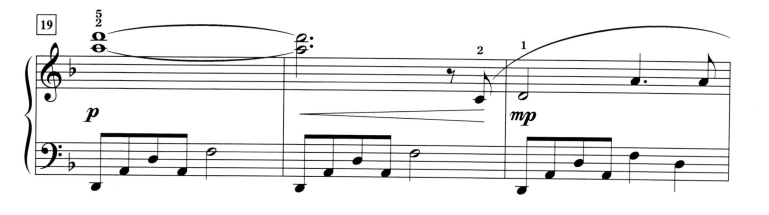

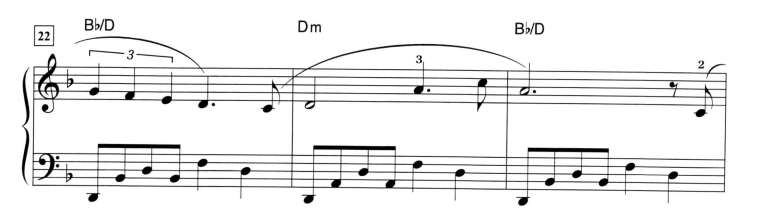

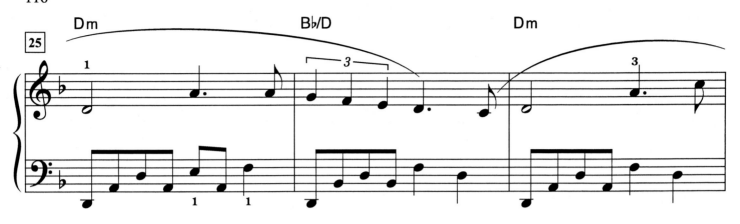

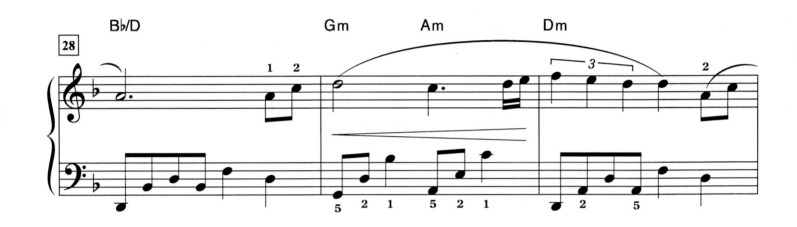

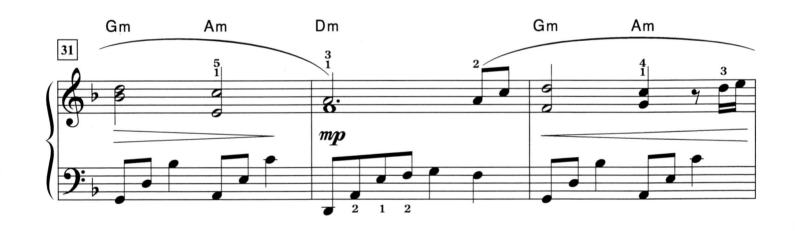

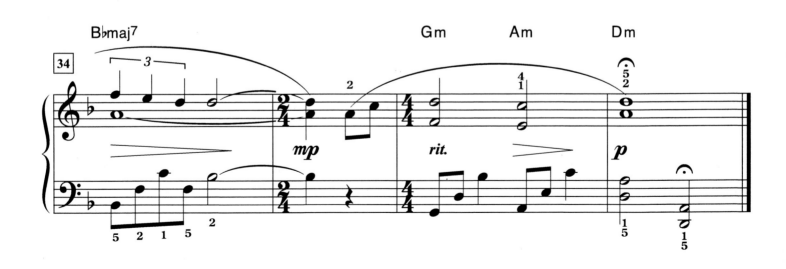

# MOVIN' ON UP

(from *The Jeffersons*)

Words and Music by
Jeff Barry and Janet Dubois
Arranged by Dan Coates

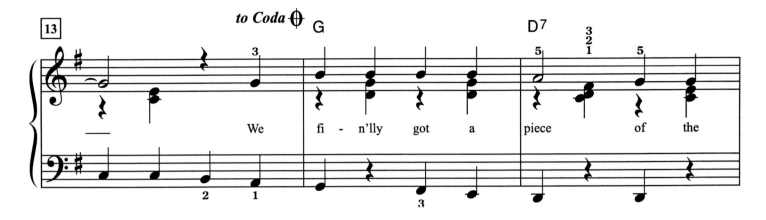

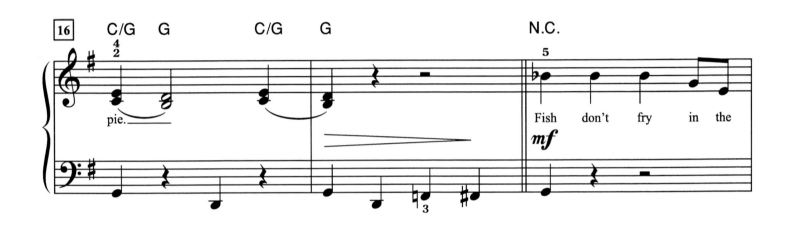

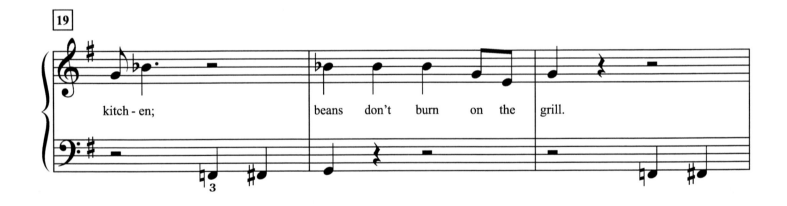

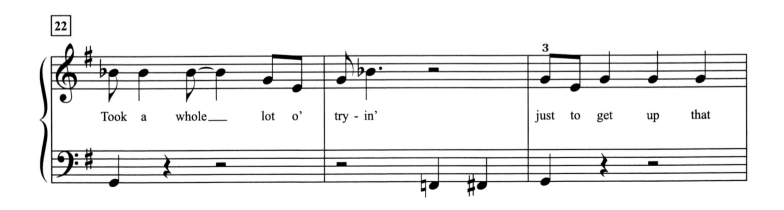

hill. Now we're up___ in the big leagues

get - tin' our turn at bat. As long as we live, it's

*cresc.*

**D7**

**D.S. al Coda**

you and me, ba - by, there ain't noth - in' wrong with that.___ Well, we're mov - in' on

*f*

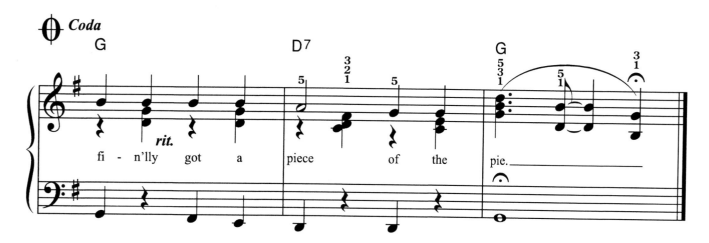

**Coda**

**G**    **D7**    **G**

fi - n'lly got a piece of the pie.___

*rit.*

# SONG FROM "M*A*S*H"

## (SUICIDE IS PAINLESS)

Words and Music by
Mike Altman and Johnny Mandel
Arranged by Dan Coates

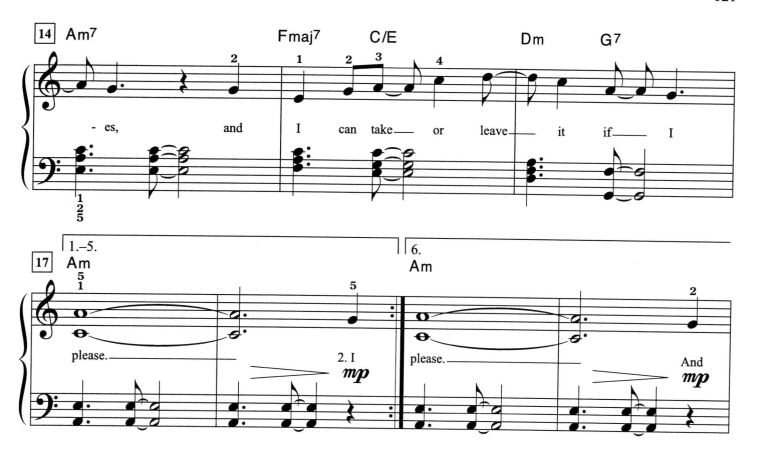

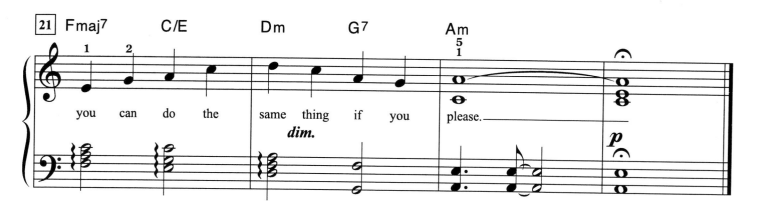

Verse 2:
I try to find a way to make
All our little joys relate
Without that ever-present hate
But now I know that it's too late.
And *(To Chorus:)*

Verse 3:
The game of life is hard to play,
I'm going to lose it anyway,
The losing card I'll someday lay,
So that is all I have to say,
That *(To Chorus:)*

Verse 4:
The only way you win is cheat,
And lay it down before I'm beat,
And to another give a seat,
For that's the only painless feat.
'Cause *(To Chorus:)*

Verse 5:
The sword of time will pierce our skins,
It doesn't hurt when it begins,
But as it works its way on in
The pain grows stronger, watch it grin.
For *(To Chorus:)*

Verse 6:
A brave man once requested me
To answer questions that are key,
Is it to be or not to be?
And I replied, "Oh, why ask me?"
'Cause *(To Chorus:)*

# THE NOTEBOOK

## (Main Title)

Written by Aaron Zigman
Arranged by Dan Coates

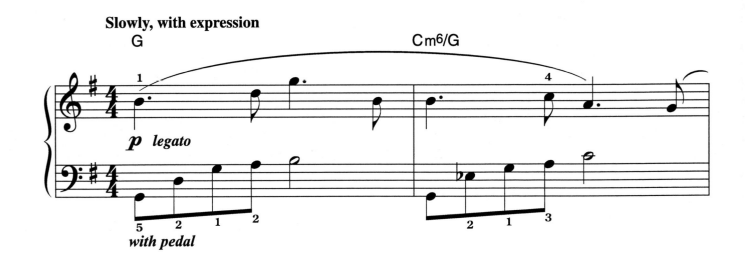

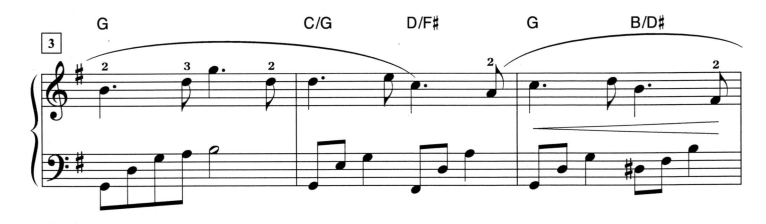

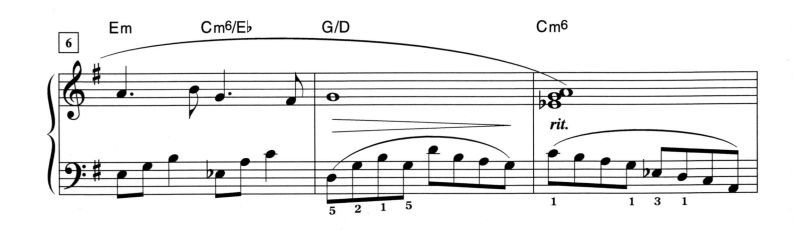

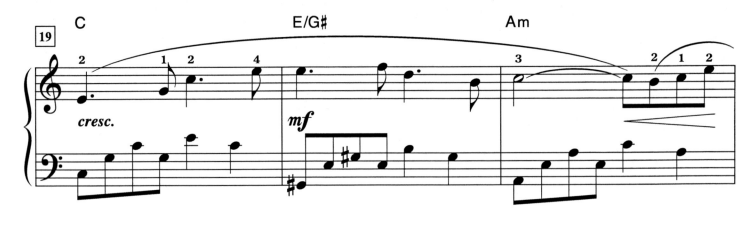

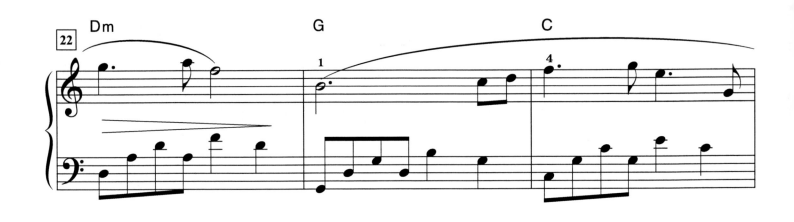

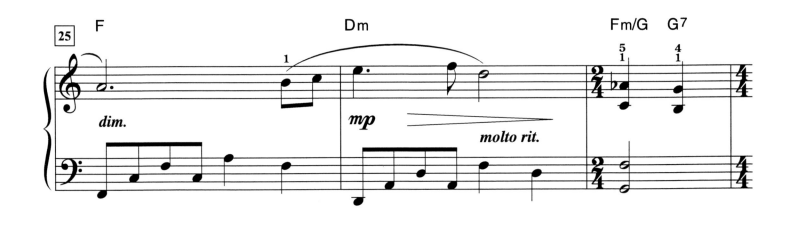

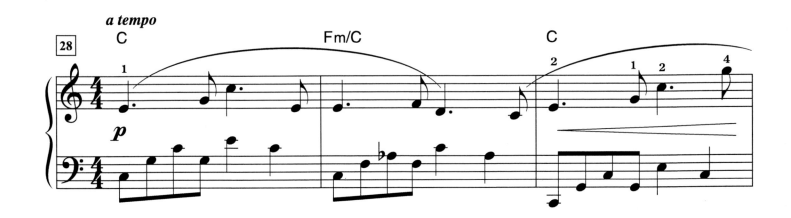

# THEME FROM *NEW YORK, NEW YORK*

(from *New York, New York*)

Music by John Kander
Words by Fred Ebb
Arranged by Dan Coates

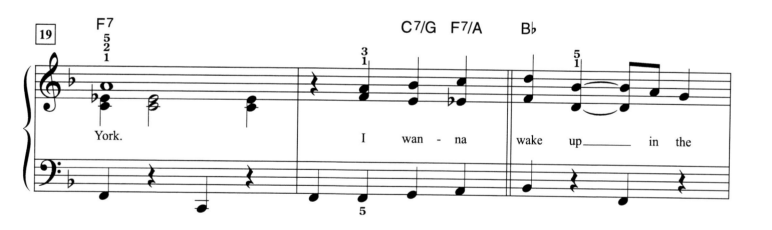

# OUT HERE ON MY OWN

## (from *Fame*)

Music by Michael Gore
Lyrics by Lesley Gore
Arranged by Dan Coates

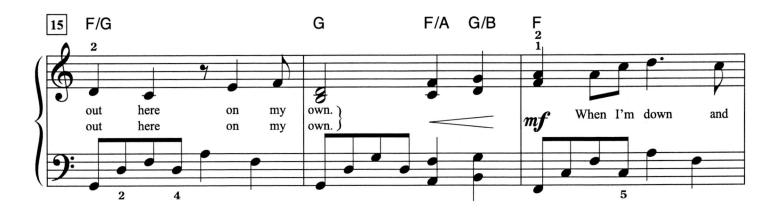

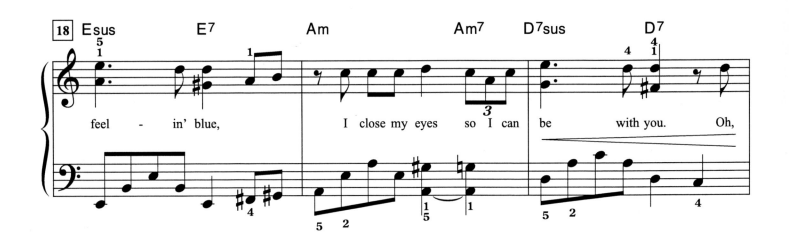

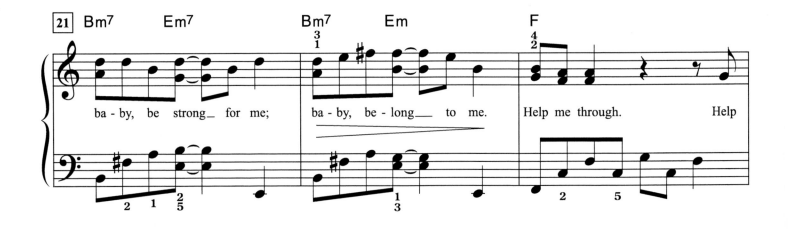

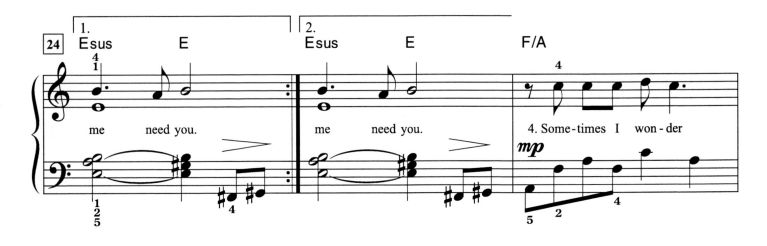

where I've been, who I am, do I fit in?

I may not win, but I can't be thrown out_____ here

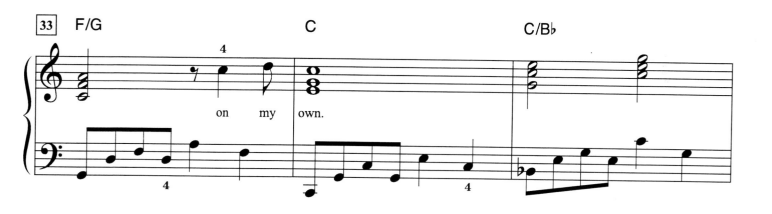

on my own.

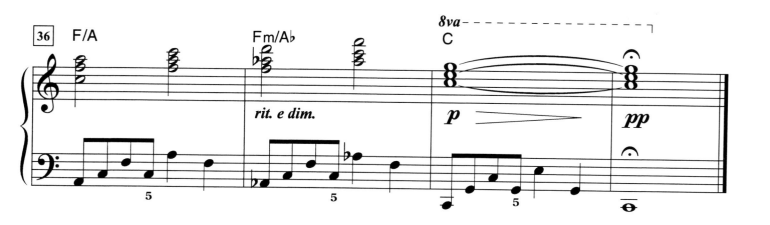

rit. e dim.

# OVER THE RAINBOW

(from *The Wizard of Oz*)

Music by Harold Arlen
Lyrics by E.Y. Harburg
Arranged by Dan Coates

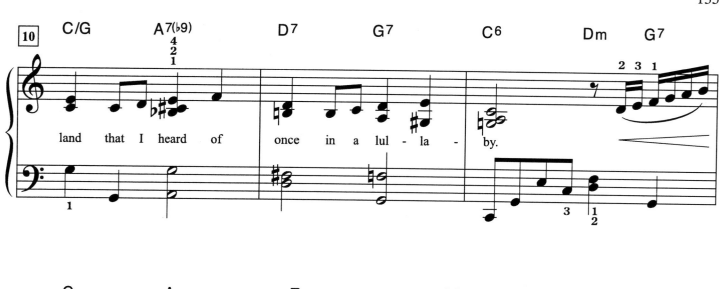

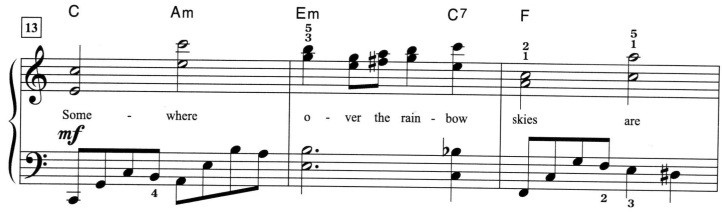

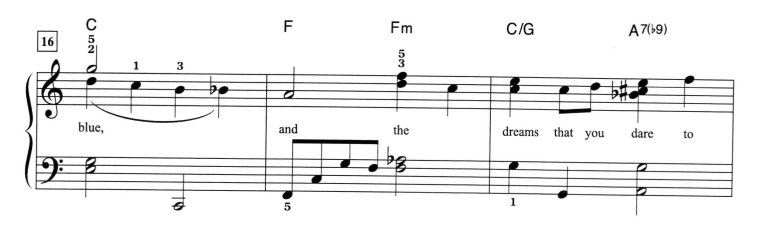

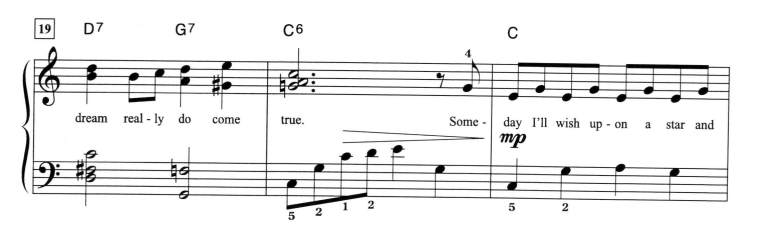

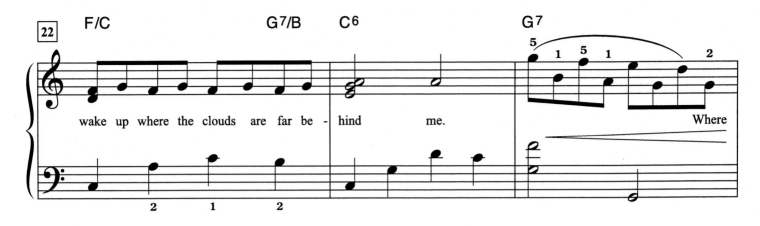

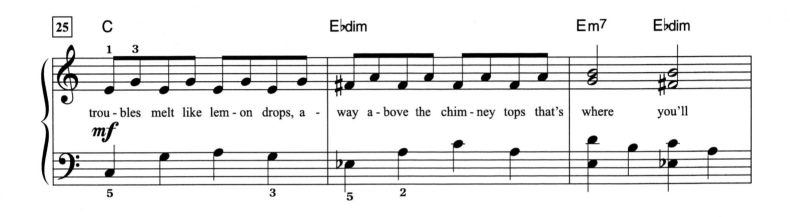

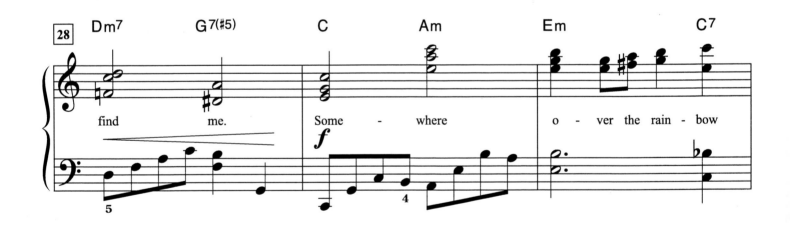

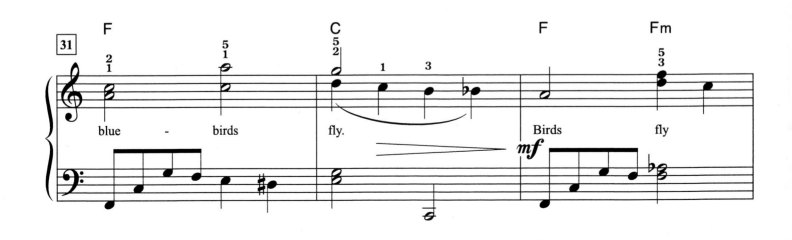

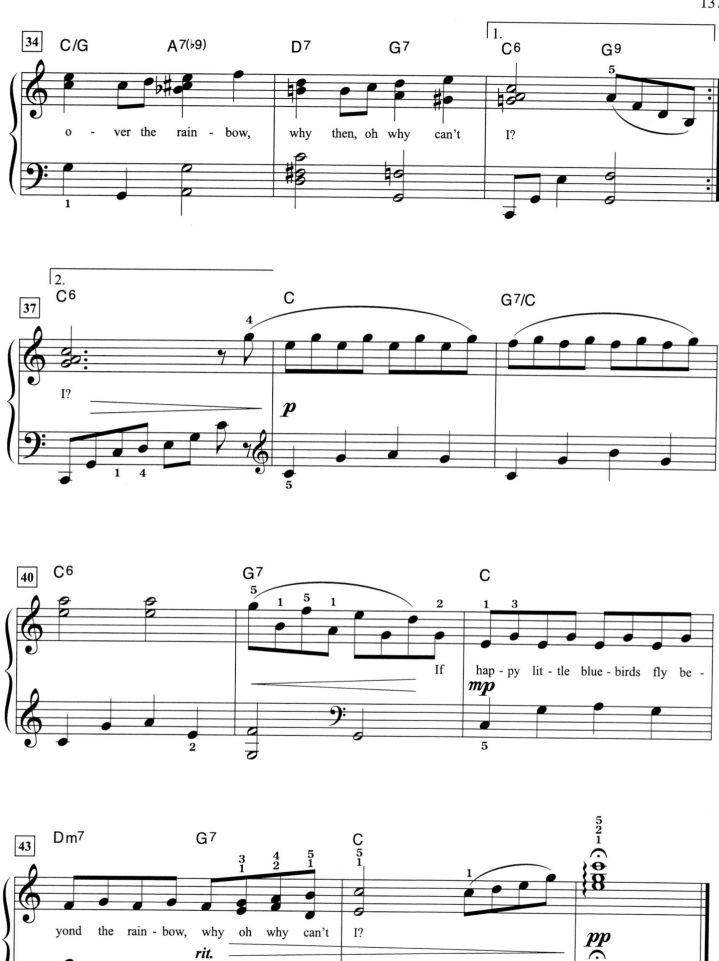

# PART OF YOUR WORLD

### (from Walt Disney's *The Little Mermaid*)

Music by Alan Menken
Lyrics by Howard Ashman
Arranged by Dan Coates

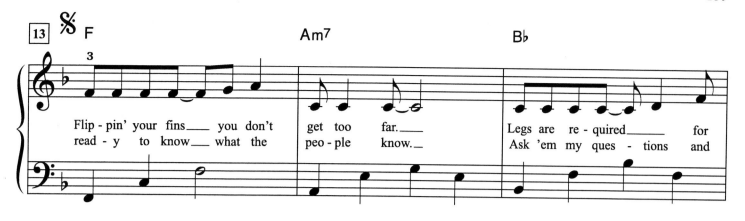

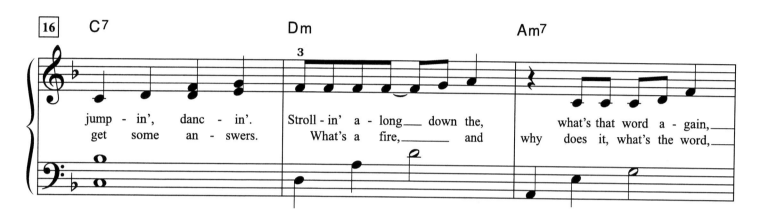

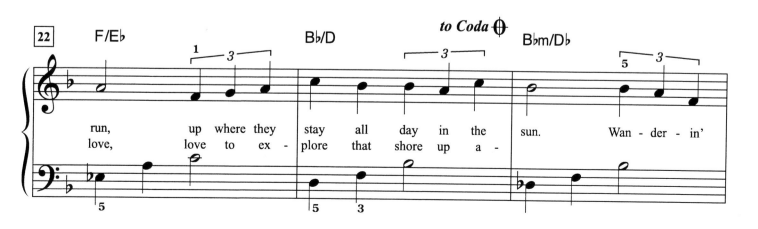

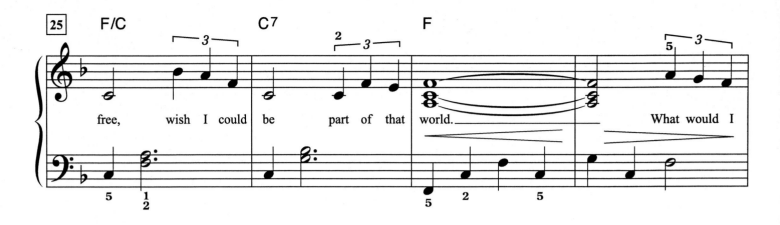

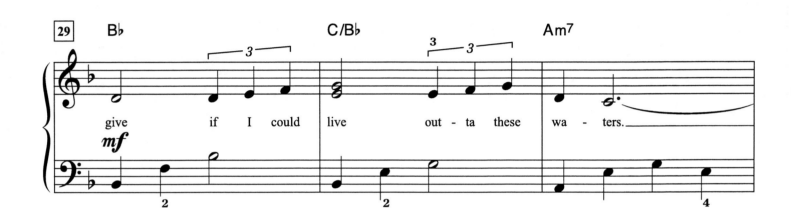

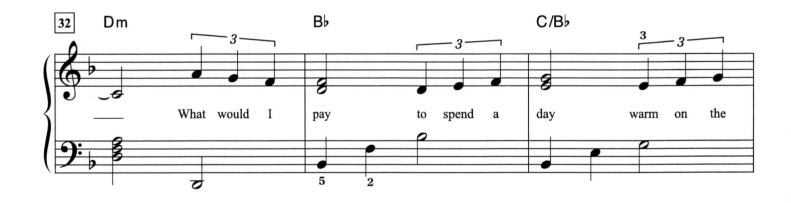

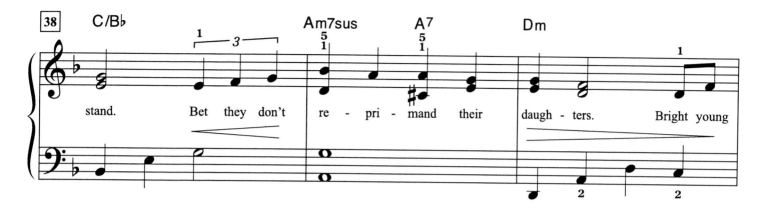

stand. Bet they don't re - pri - mand their daugh - ters. Bright young

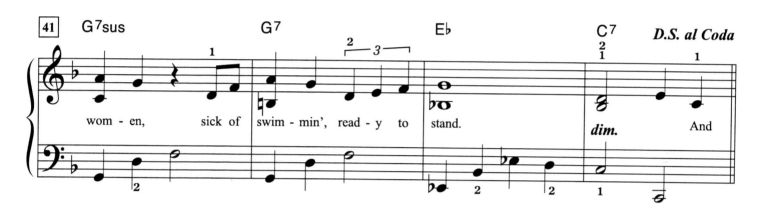

wom - en, sick of swim - min', read - y to stand. *dim.* And

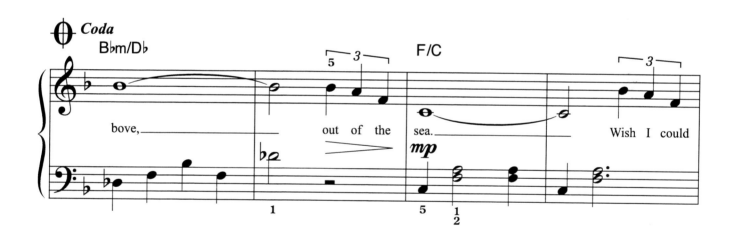

bove, out of the sea. Wish I could

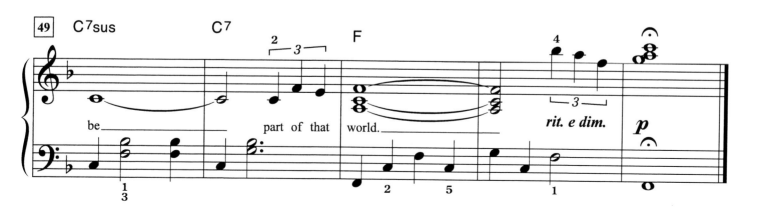

be part of that world. *rit. e dim.*

# THE PINK PANTHER

(from *The Pink Panther*)

By Henry Mancini
Arranged by Dan Coates

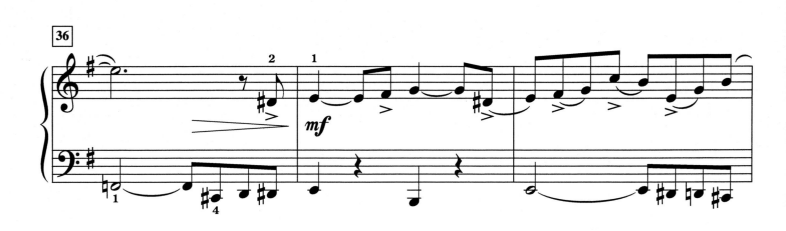

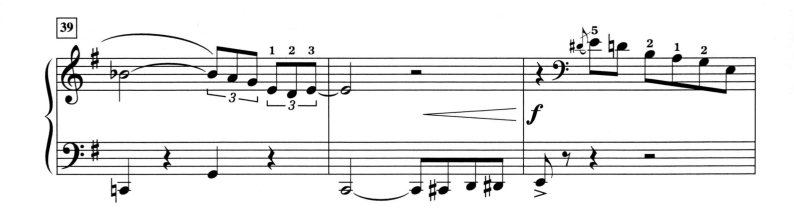

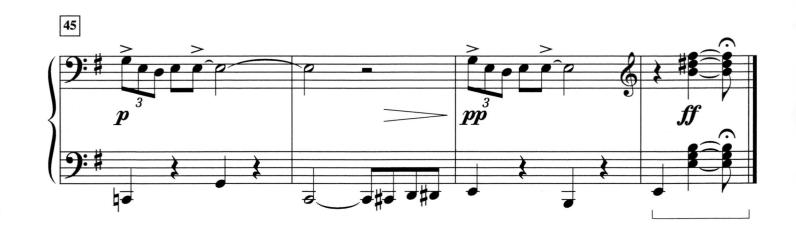

# PRINCESS LEIA'S THEME

(from *Star Wars*)

Music by John Williams
Arranged by Dan Coates

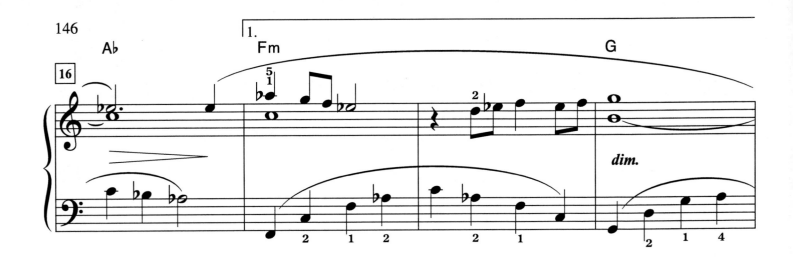

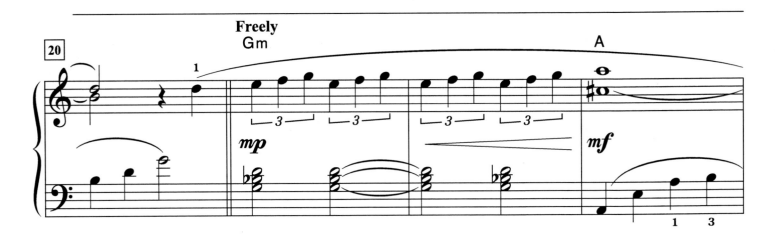

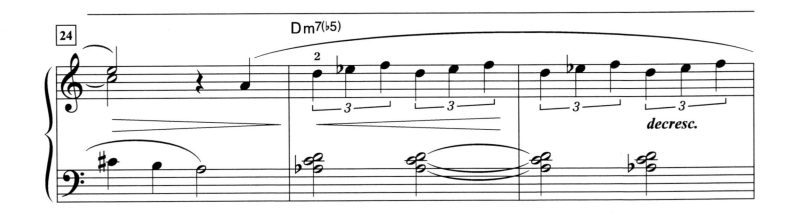

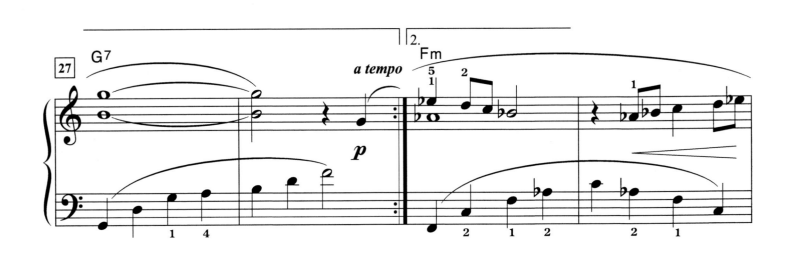

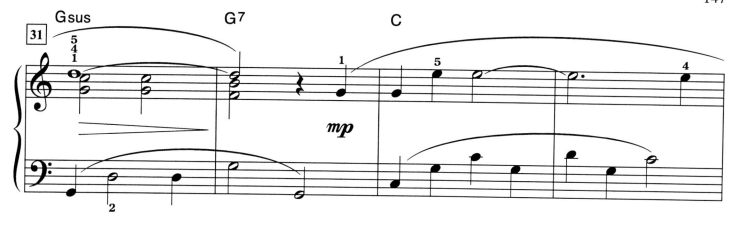

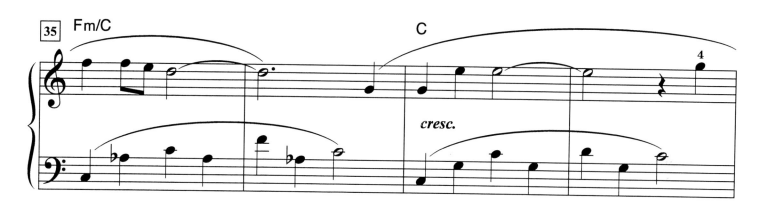

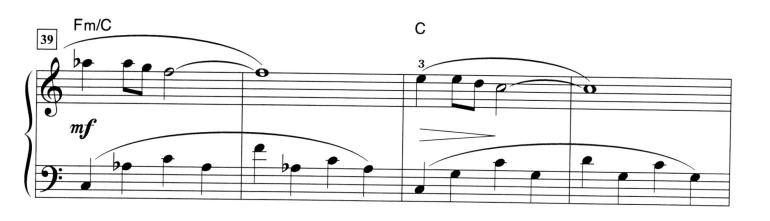

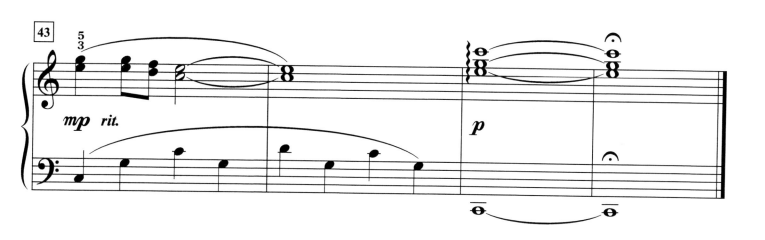

# RAIDERS MARCH

## (from *Raiders of the Lost Ark*)

Music by John Williams
Arranged by Dan Coates

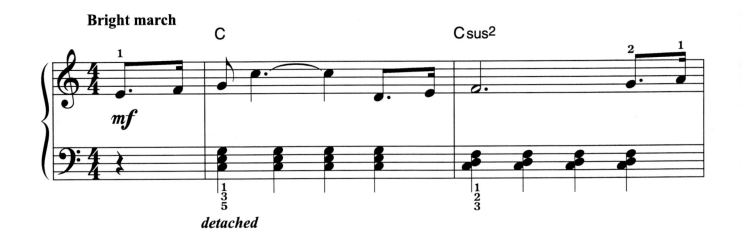

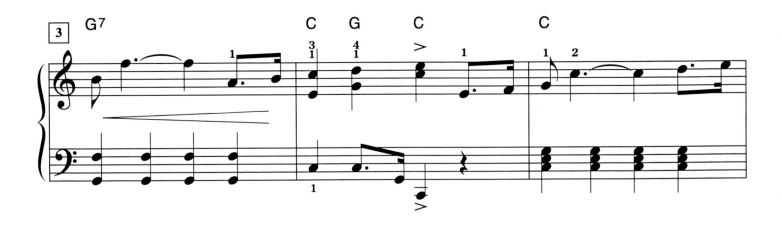

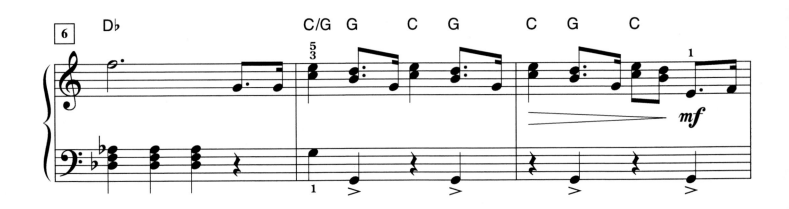

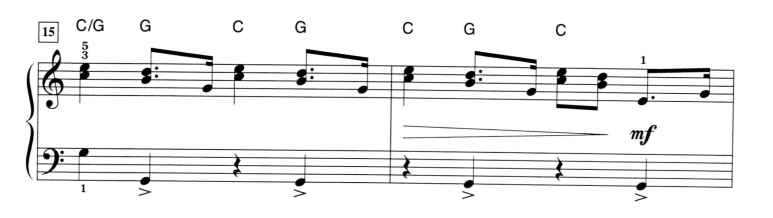

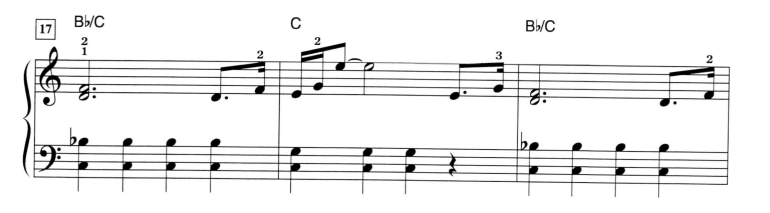

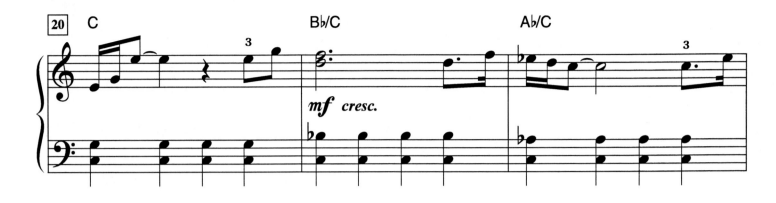

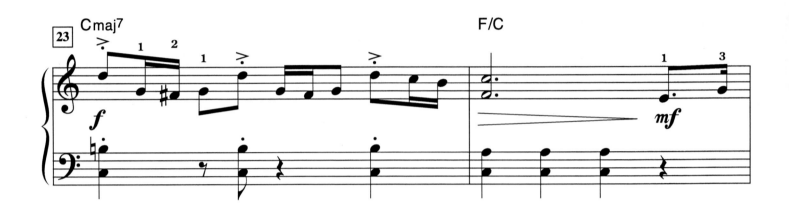

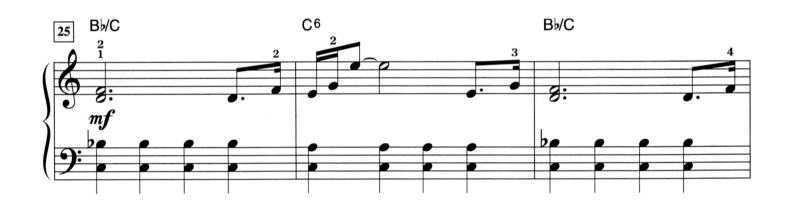

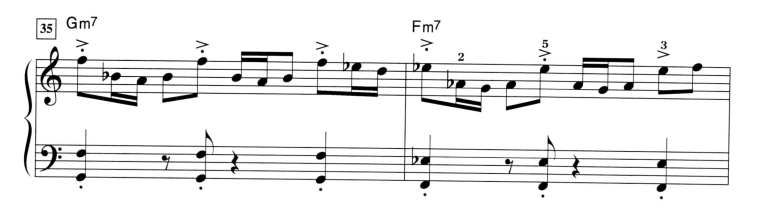

# THE ROSE

(from *The Rose*)

Words and Music by
Amanda McBroom
Arranged by Dan Coates

# SECONDHAND WHITE BABY GRAND

(from *SMASH*)

Lyrics by Scott Wittman and Marc Shaiman
Music by Marc Shaiman
Arranged by Dan Coates

give._____ For man-y years____ the mu-sic had____ to

roam_____ un-til we found a way____ to find____ a

home._____ 3. So, now I wake up ev-'ry day and

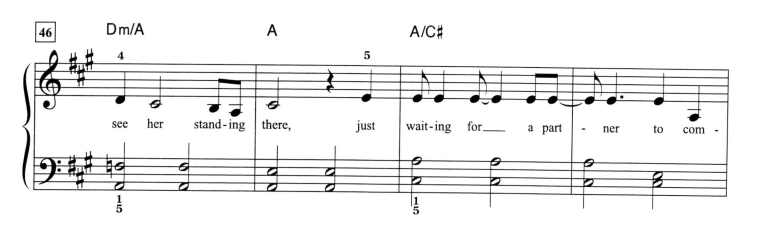

see her stand-ing there, just wait-ing for____ a part-ner to com-

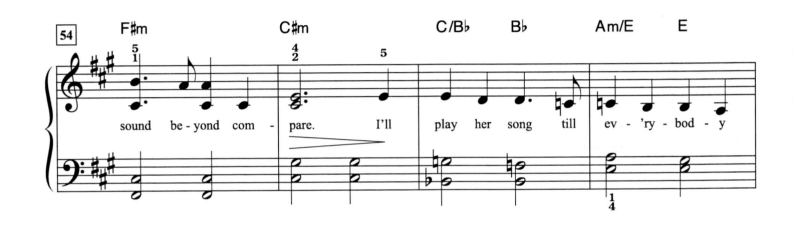

*Chorus:*

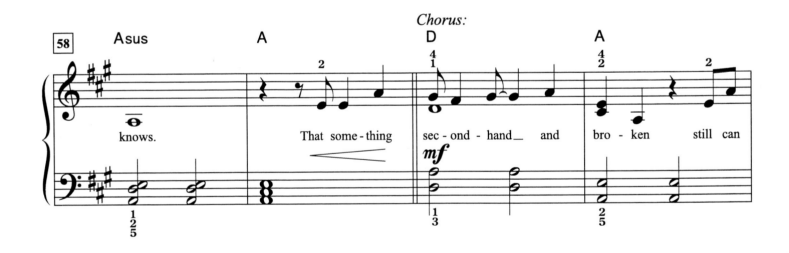

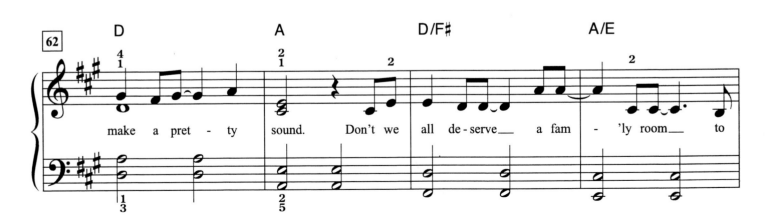

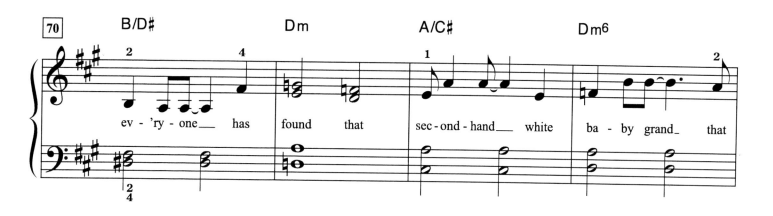

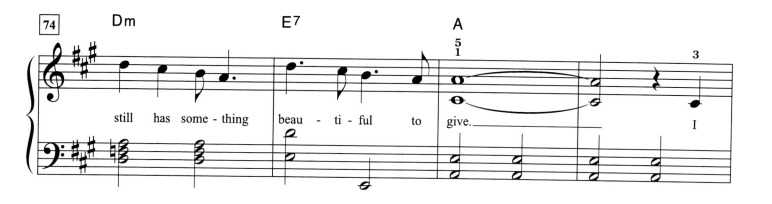

# STAR WARS

## (MAIN THEME)

Music by John Williams
Arranged by Dan Coates

# STAYIN' ALIVE

## (from *Saturday Night Fever*)

Words and Music by
Barry Gibb, Maurice Gibb and Robin Gibb
Arranged by Dan Coates

**Moderate rock beat, in two**

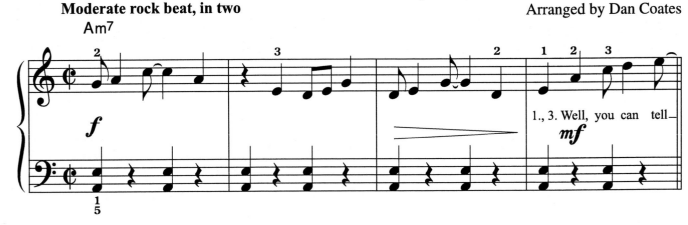

# SINGIN' IN THE RAIN

(from *Singin' in the Rain*)

Music by Nacio Herb Brown
Lyric by Arthur Freed
Arranged by Dan Coates

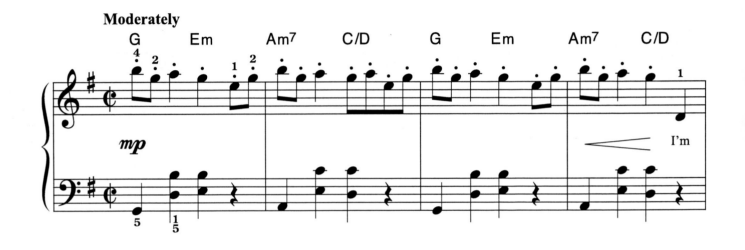

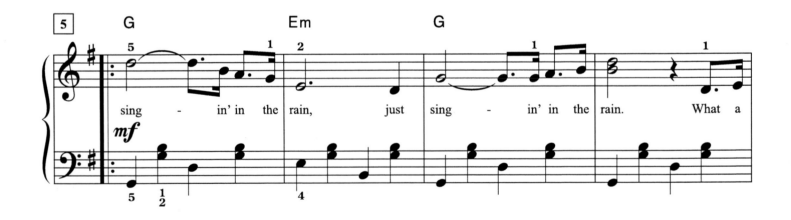

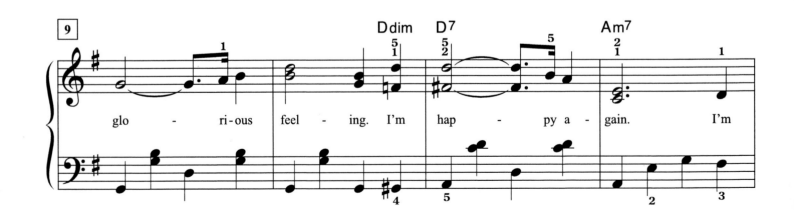

laugh - ing at clouds so dark up a - bove, the

sun's in my heart and I'm read - y for love. Let the

storm - y clouds chase ev - 'ry - one from the place.

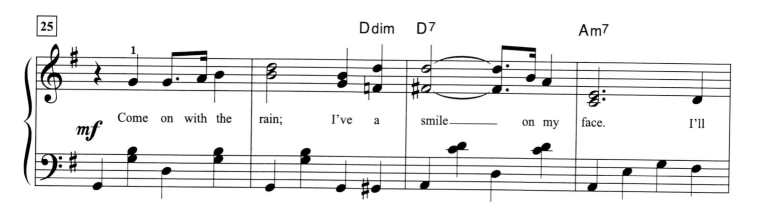

Come on with the rain; I've a smile on my face. I'll

walk down the lane with a hap - py re - frain, and

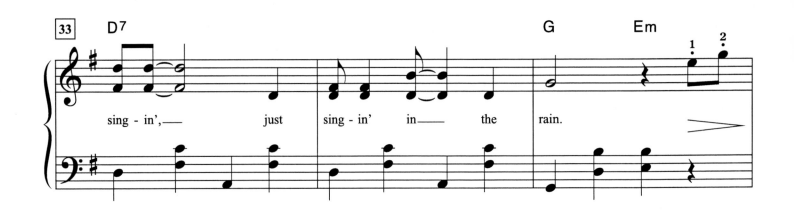

sing - in', just sing - in' in the rain.

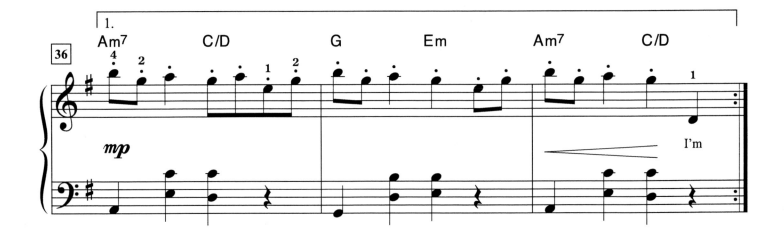

I'm

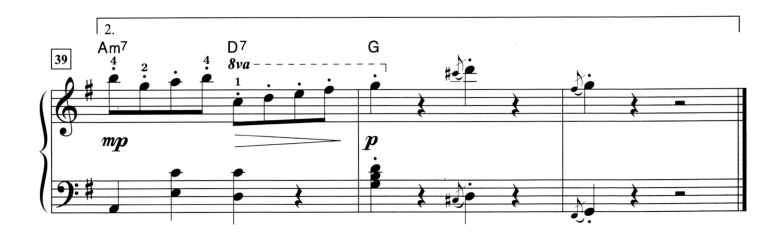

# THOSE WERE THE DAYS

## (from *All in the Family*)

Music by Charles Strouse
Words by Lee Adams
Arranged by Dan Coates

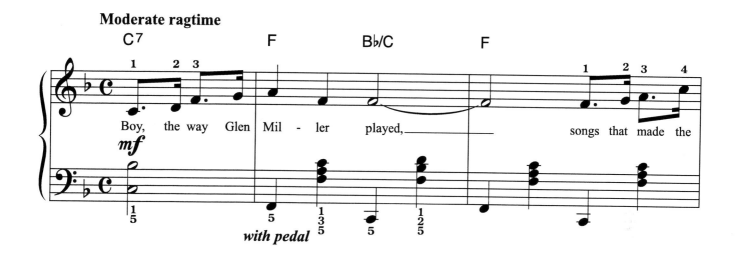

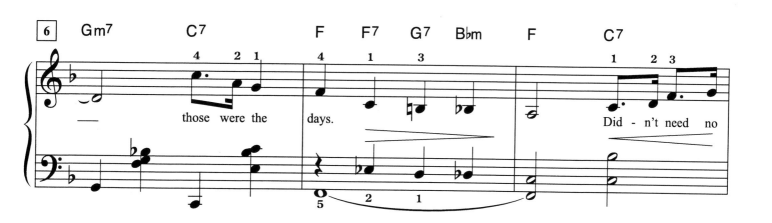

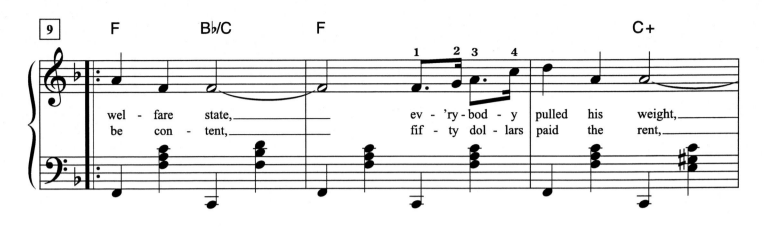

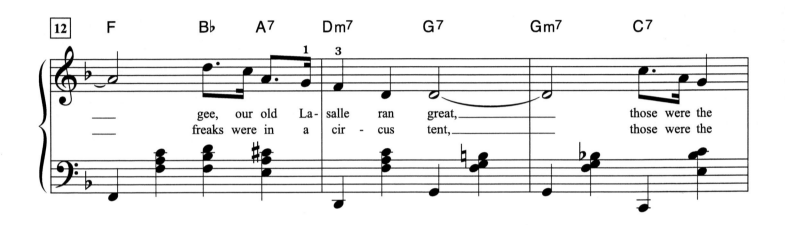

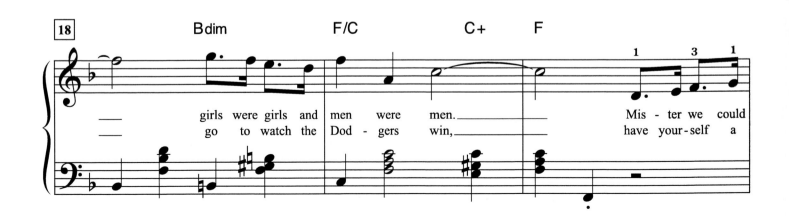

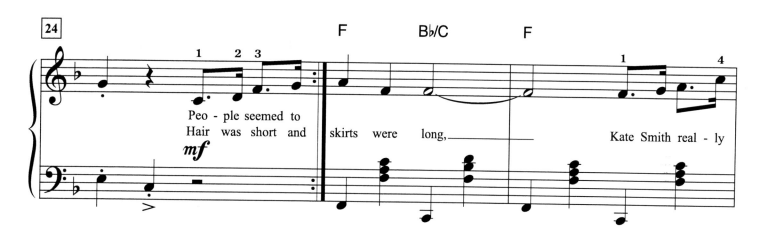

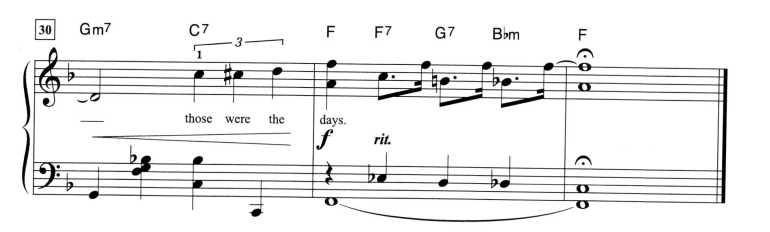

# THE WIND BENEATH MY WINGS

## (from *Beaches*)

Words and Music by
Larry Henley and Jeff Silbar
Arranged by Dan Coates

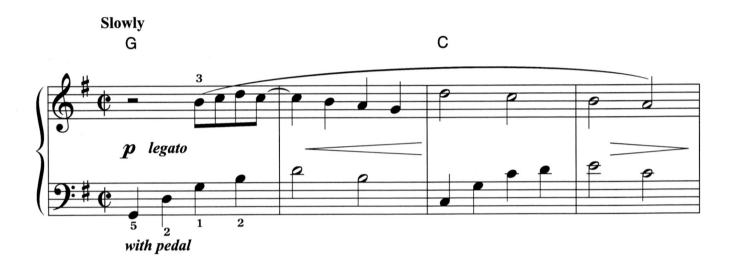

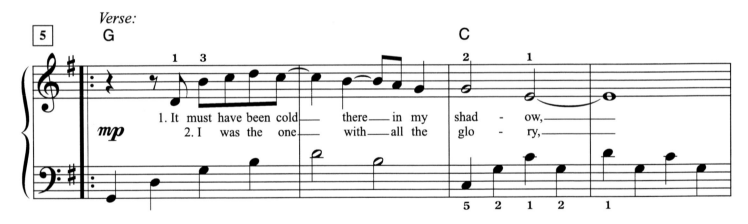

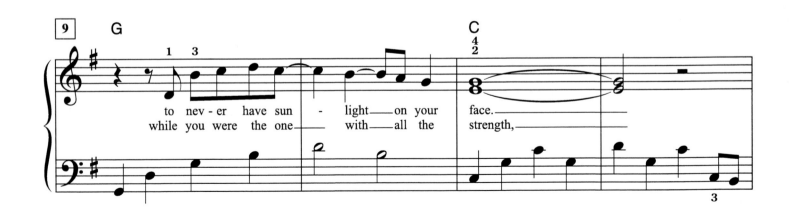

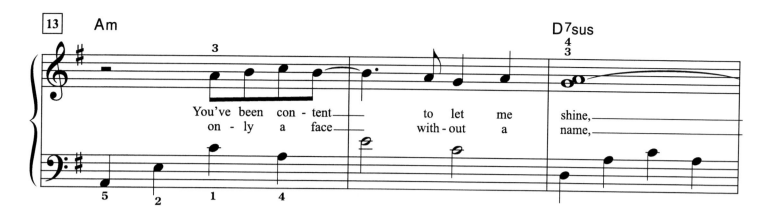

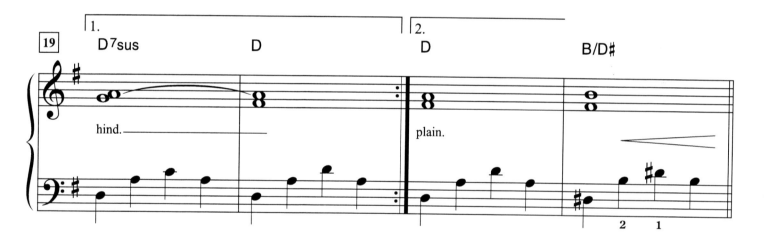

# YOU HAVEN'T SEEN THE LAST OF ME

(from *Burlesque*)

Words and Music by
Diane Warren
Arranged by Dan Coates

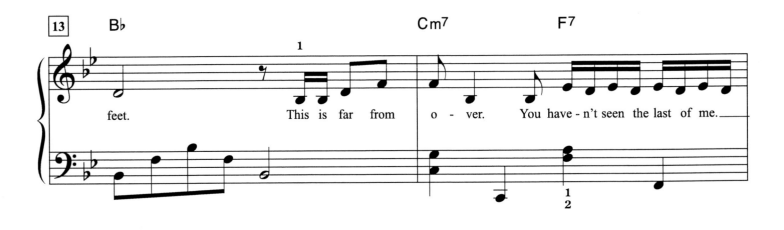

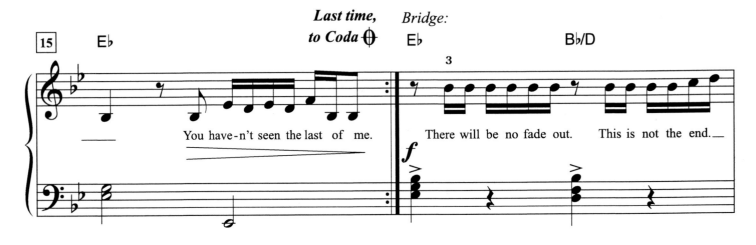

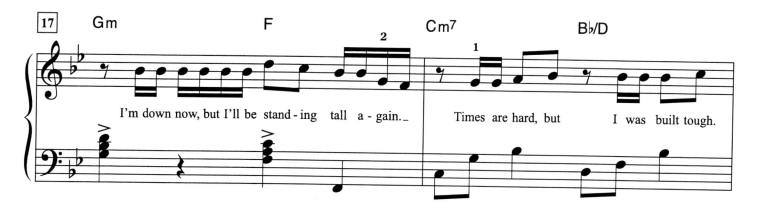

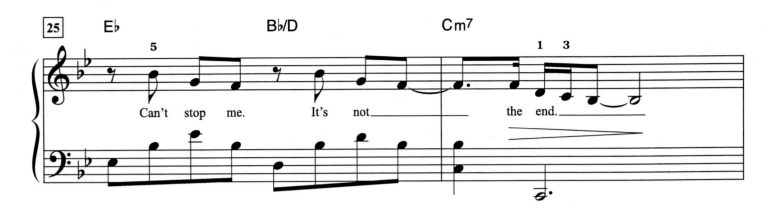

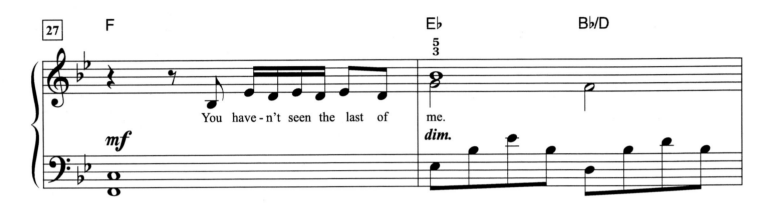

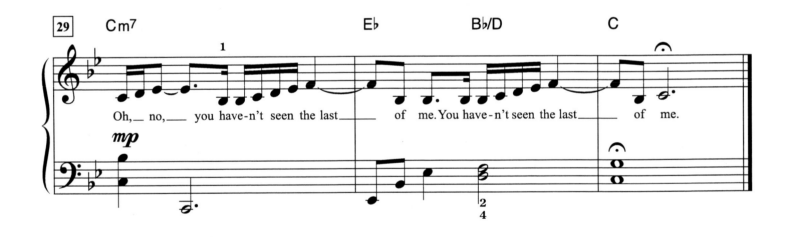

*Verse 2:*
They can say that I won't stay around,
But I'm gonna stand my ground.
You're not gonna stop me.
You don't know me, you don't know who I am.
Don't count me out so fast.
*(To Chorus:)*

# YOU'VE GOT A FRIEND IN ME

(from *Toy Story*)

Words and Music by
by Randy Newman
Arranged by Dan Coates

nice warm bed,—— you just re-mem-ber what your old pal said,—— boy,

you've got a friend in me.—— Yeah, you've got a friend in me.

cresc.

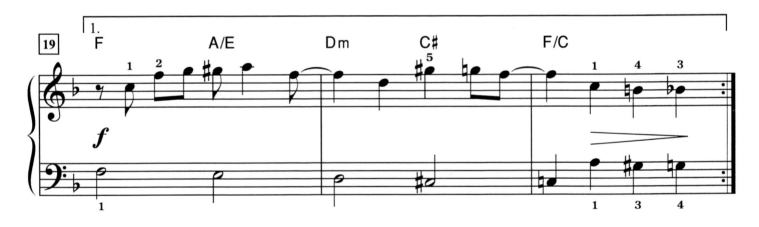

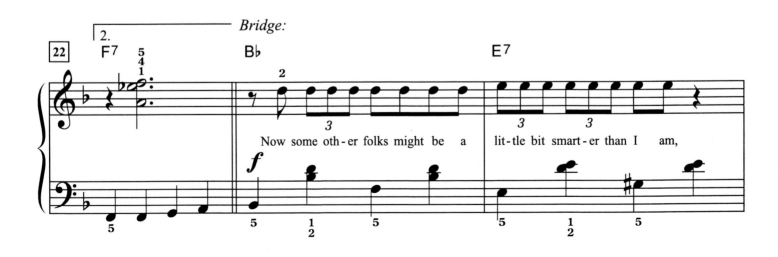

Now some oth-er folks might be a lit-tle bit smart-er than I am,

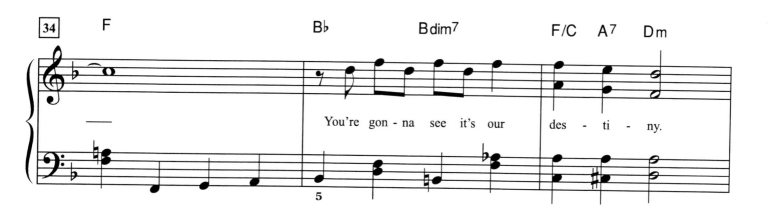

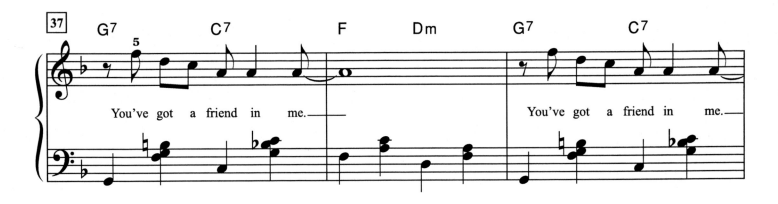

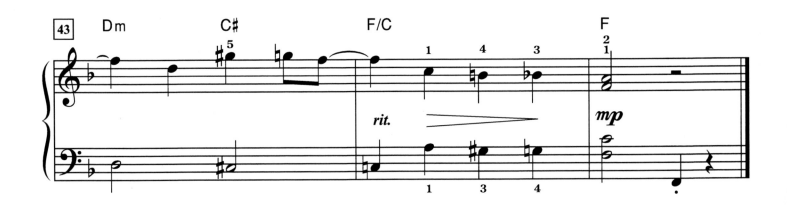

*Verse 2:*
You've got a friend in me.
You've got a friend in me.
You got troubles, then I got 'em, too.
There isn't anything I wouldn't do for you.
If we stick together we can see it through,
'Cause you've got a friend in me.
Yeah, you've got a friend in me.

# A WHOLE NEW WORLD

## (from Walt Disney's *Aladdin*)

Words by Tim Rice
Music by Alan Menken
Arranged by Dan Coates

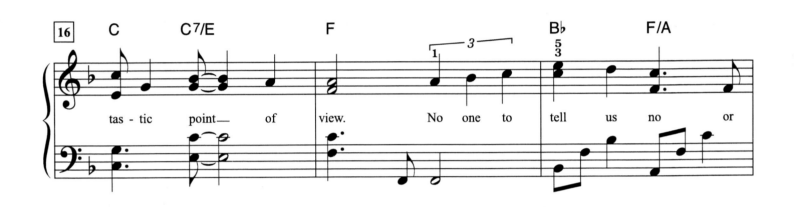

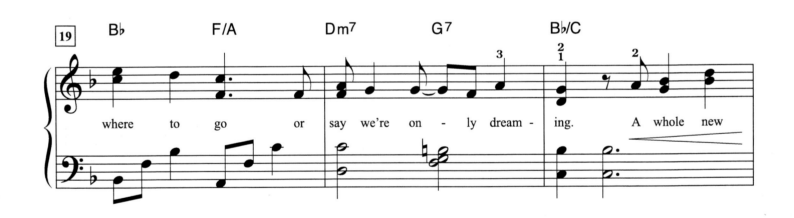

# THEME FROM "SUPERMAN"

Music by John Williams
Arranged by Dan Coates

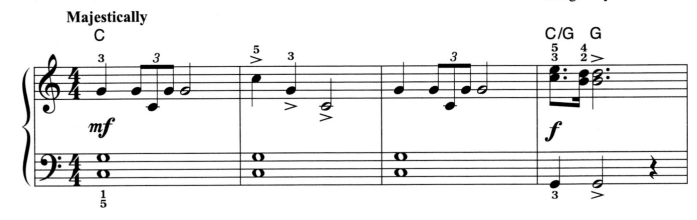

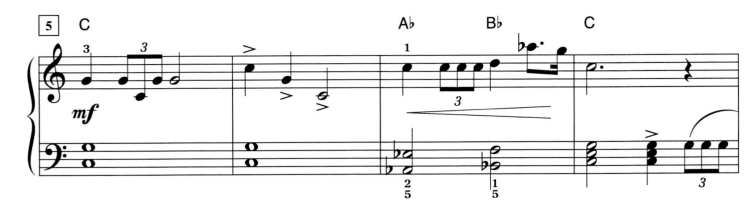

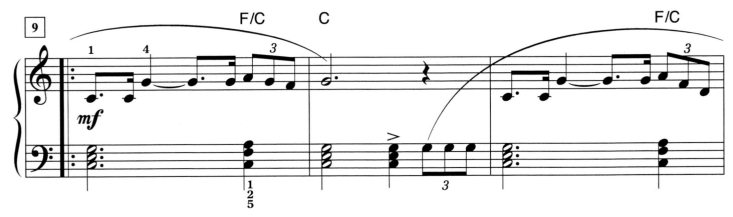

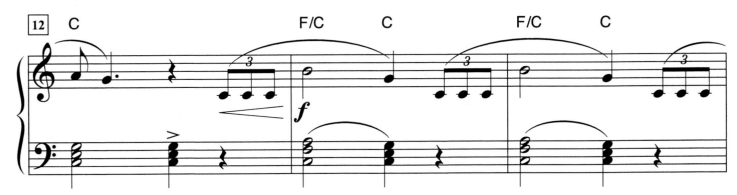

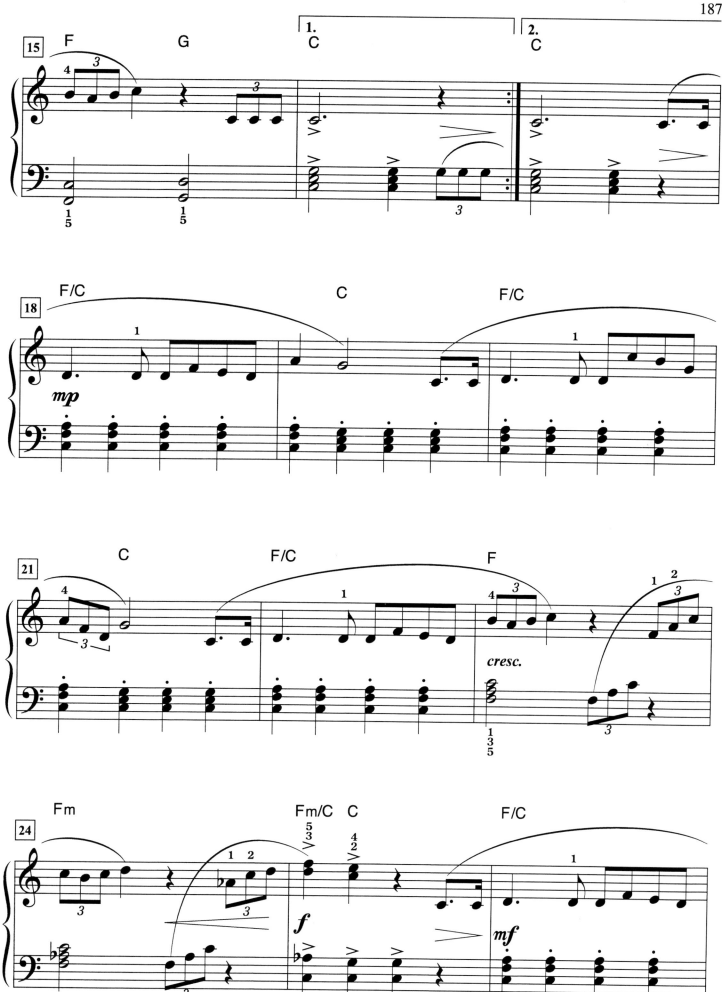